Enrollment Simulation and Planning

Enrollment Simulation and Planning

Chuck McIntyre

COMMUNITY COLLEGE PRESS®

a division of the American Association of
Community Colleges

Washington, D.C.

The American Association of Community Colleges (AACC) is the primary advocacy organization for the nation's community colleges. The association represents 1,100 two-year, associate degree-granting institutions and some 10 million students. AACC provides leadership and service in five key areas: policy initiatives, advocacy, research, education services, and coordination/networking.

©1999 American Association of Community Colleges

Requests for permission should be sent to
Community College Press
American Association of Community Colleges
One Dupont Circle, NW
Suite 410
Washington, DC 20036
Fax: (202) 223-9390

Printed in the United States of America.

ISBN 0-87117-322-0

For a free catalog of Community College Press® publications or to place an order, please call (800) 250-6557.

Contents

Figures

Tables

Preface

Although current literature on community colleges calls for revolutionary changes, the ideas are based mostly on changes in information technology and greater relevance of curriculum. Few of the calls contain specific information for institutional planners about how to quantify or present a range of likely future scenarios and how to translate these scenarios into potential enrollment, preferred policies, and practices—in other words, how to get there from here.

Many analytical techniques and timesaving computer software packages are available for enrollment planning, but they do not appear to be widely used by community college chief executive officers and managers. George Schmidtlein (1990) and others suggest that effective planning and change are constrained by the neglect of important aspects of a college's decision making. According to Schmidtlein, planners too often fail to integrate multiple planning processes for curriculum, student services, operating budgets, and facilities. Keller (1983) argues that college planners need to integrate scientific and political

approaches more often without neglecting either. Peter Drucker (1967) argues that managers do not pay enough attention to the entrepreneurial (risk-taking) aspects of planning, a point that appears even more relevant today as community colleges are confronted by expanding numbers of competitors and by changing instructional delivery.

The recent Computer-Aided Planning (CAP) project illustrates the difficulties of applying existing tools to the needs of college strategic planning. The project, which was conducted in collaboration with 40 community colleges in the United States, Canada, and the United Kingdom, was intended to develop simulation models to support institutional planning and decision making. Descriptions by Paul Brinkman, Kurt Groninga, and Chuck McIntyre (1994) and by Brinkman, McIntyre, and Trische Robertson (1995) show how decisions were studied, models built, and simple and sustainable software applications selected for the CAP project.

Although the CAP project researchers found that it was possible to build relatively powerful but low-cost "expert system" models to support college planning, the actual use of the CAP products has been problematic for five reasons:

- Priority is typically given to operations first, to management second, and only then to planning.

- The data required by the models are plentiful, but not consistent or readily accessible.

- Staff change frequently.

- Software platforms and applications change continually.

- College planning processes typically involve staff "buy-in," but just as typically ignore the use of tools such as expert systems, simulation models, and statistical estimation techniques.

A possible solution to the nominal use of planning tools is to concentrate on a key issue—such as student enrollment trends—and build models that enable college staff to simulate and plan for future enrollment. This solution makes sense because effective strategic planning for community colleges should emphasize the number and kinds of students the college will enroll in the future and what kinds of education they will need.

A college can manage some of the factors that affect future enrollments, including tuition, fees, curriculum, services, and delivery methods. Factors that a college cannot manage, but must be able to predict, include market population, economic and social trends, actions of other providers, and public policies. Therefore, a college's future external environment must be described—a major component of strategic planning—and set against the policies and practices the college may employ in the future.

This task lends itself to the approach that is the focus of this book: enrollment simulation and planning (ESP). This approach is centered around the use of statistical models to describe how and why college enrollments fluctuate. College planners may use this approach with confidence to simulate any number of plausible future scenarios. Planners can then set a variety of possible college actions (policies and practices) against those scenarios, and examine the results of projected future enrollments for their planning implications.

This book begins with an introduction that explains three lines of inquiry—futures research, enrollment determination, and enrollment management—that provide conceptual background for ESP and help to highlight the differences between manageable and unmanageable factors. Throughout the book, examples are presented to illustrate the ESP model. The examples are from case studies, but college names have been replaced with generic names such as County Community College or Metro Community College. State and county names have also been replaced with generic labeling for the purpose of the examples.

Part 1, "Studying Enrollment," begins with ways to identify a community college's key enrollment trends (chapter 1), and how to use ESP statistical models to explain the causes of these trends (chapter 2). Once collegewide enrollment trends are explained for both short- and long-term periods, analysts can then use similar methods to explain the enrollment behavior of specific kinds of students (chapter 3).

After explaining the college's past enrollment fluctuations, another perspective is examined and ESP tools are employed to specify the impact on enrollment of factors within the college's control (chapter 4) and outside the college's control (chapter 5).

To complete the enrollment picture, the focus is changed to the college's market penetration. Chapter 6 analyzes the extent to which a college enrolls those in its service area; chapter 7 examines the extent to which a college *should* enroll those in its service area. The difference between these two measures provides a point of departure for identifying desired changes in those factors—policies and practices—that the college controls.

But, how is it known that the changes will have their intended effects, given that some important determinants of enrollments are outside the college's control? This is where ESP can be most useful and is addressed in part 2, "Forecasting, Simulating, and Planning." To look at a range of different but possible scenarios,

chapter 8 shows how the work in part 1 can be refined into a forecasting model and how to use that model for enrollment simulations. Chapter 9 discusses how to develop a useful baseline scenario, that is, one that is plausible.

Chapter 10 examines the process of constructing other scenarios from a number of "what if" questions. Since the future is largely unpredictable, the best approach is to define a reasonable range of possible scenarios. Chapter 11 covers the significance of basic trends and wild cards.

A college can plan strategically only if it is aware of external trends and assesses their implications. Chapter 12 ends the book with a review of how a college can apply ESP in its planning, evaluation, and decision making.

Acknowledgments

I would like to thank my wife, Donna; my sons, Scott, Todd, and Eric; and my daughters-in-law, Vicky and Nancy, for their remarkable patience and support of my work, especially over the past decade, as I have undertaken a variety of projects, some of which proved to be quite time-consuming. None of my efforts would have been possible without their support.

Further, a fond acknowledgment of two colleagues, Paul Brinkman and Trische Robertson, whose patience, sage advice, and marvelously cooperative working styles have been a tremendous help to me in recent years. And, I can't begin to measure the value of their friendship.

Also deserving of thanks are the staff at the many community colleges that participated in the CAP project between 1990 and 1995, and especially the staff at the colleges that were subject, more recently, to the experiments in thinking that led to many of the ideas contained herein: Maricopa, Pima, Lansing, Portland, Mt. Hood, and Lane Community Colleges. My colleagues at the California state chancellor's office have been most helpful, as well.

Finally, thanks to Margaret Rivera and Donna Carey at the American Association of Community Colleges, who have been very supportive of my work on this document.

Introduction

Enrollment simulation and planning (ESP) is the use of statistical modeling to forecast, simulate, and plan for future community college enrollments. ESP involves using an environmental scan to identify relevant future scenarios that provide the data necessary to run the models, then using the results of this modeling to develop plans for college policy and practice.

The most important considerations for ESP are the changes in enrollment and market penetration at a college over time, and comparisons of the college's market penetration with that of other, similar, colleges. College staff should establish a range of likely college futures and compare them with existing expectations to develop and prioritize strategies for making changes in curriculum, services, budget, staffing, and facilities. In subsequent planning and in the development of new strategies, the actual results of implemented strategies can be contrasted with the predicted results. This work brings together three lines of inquiry and analysis.

The first line of inquiry is futures research, or *environmental scanning*. One of the initial steps of college planning, environmental scanning involves identifying the conditions that might occur in a college's service area or across its constituency. Such possible conditions are generally categorized around demographics, economics, culture, technology, and public policy. Descriptions of possible conditions are most usefully cast in trend scenarios whose likelihood can be assessed. This is just the first step. The real task is to assess the implications of these possible futures for the college.

The second line of inquiry is *enrollment determination*. This body of work and literature, reviewed by Brinkman and McIntyre (1997), uses a variety of models, both qualitative and quantitative, to identify the factors that are important in determining college and university enrollment. Curve-fitting and causal models are employed to quantify the relationships among enrollment, tuition, fees, and financial aid. Forecasting most often involves curve-fitting, an approach that assumes—nearly always incorrectly—that conditions in and out of the institution will remain the same. The importance of many factors, not just one, in determining enrollment and the virtual certainty that conditions will change call for the use of a causal model like the statistical regression proposed in this work.

The third line of inquiry is *enrollment management*, which involves the steps that colleges and universities can take to reduce, stabilize, increase, or change the mix of their enrollments. Although much of the advice in this area concerns micromanagement (marketing, scheduling, retention, etc.), Michael Dolence (1993) has expanded the scope of enrollment management to include the implications of factors external to the institution and has renamed it *strategic enrollment management* (SEM). Many colleges and universities use SEM as part of their package of decision-support and database software applications. SEM embodies a different procedure than the ESP recommended in this book.

In a review of the literature, Brinkman and McIntyre (1997) describe the factors that affect student enrollment, some of which the institution can manage, some of which it cannot:

Manageable

- ◆ Tuition, fees, and local financial aid
- ◆ Curriculum
- ◆ Quality, relevance, and services
- ◆ Campus sites and campus climate
- ◆ Marketing, admissions, registration, probation, dismissal

Unmanageable

- ◆ Demographics (service area population by age, gender, and ethnicity)
- ◆ Economics (service area employment, household income)
- ◆ Social and cultural trends
- ◆ Actions of other providers (tuition and fees, admissions policies)
- ◆ Public policy (federal student financial aid, tax law changes)

The importance of both manageable and unmanageable factors to college enrollment can be sorted by the statistical technique proposed in the ESP process. This tool, in conjunction with other time series analyses and comparisons of market penetration (enrollment divided by service area population) is used first to help explain why a college's enrollment fluctuates. Changes at a college or system of colleges over time are most important to this explanation. Differences from other similar community colleges are also important, but less so because of the difficulty in establishing comparability.

Following this explanation, the statistical model is refined and extended to serve as a forecasting and simulation tool for planning. This step requires that future scenarios be developed, applying the usual environmental scanning techniques but with measurable parameters.

Community colleges typically have most of the enrollment, program, and fiscal data required for the model. (See appendix A, page 61, for ESP data requirements.) A wealth of data about colleges are available over the Internet from the Web pages of individual colleges, state-level governing and coordinating agencies, and national agencies such as the National Center for Education Statistics and the American Association of Community Colleges. External data on service area demographics, economics, and culture are readily available from public and private agencies, increasingly over the Internet. Information about other institutions that provide education similar to the education offered by community colleges, especially those that operate electronically, is more difficult to obtain. The values should be input for data in cases where they are missing, provided that this step enhances, rather than diminishes, study analyses. In all cases, knowledgeable college staff can provide useful ideas, reactions, and leads.

Although the charts in this book are based on actual data, fictitious names (such as County Community College) are substituted for college names, and generic labels (such as A, 2, and c) are substituted for actual state, campus, and county names.

Part 1
Studying Enrollment

CHAPTER ONE

What Are the College's Important Enrollment Trends?

This chapter presents a way of determining a college's important enrollment trends, relying largely on data for student counts over an extended period of years, for specific categories of students.

Most community colleges experienced a period of rapid growth from the mid-1960s to the mid-1970s, followed first by a decade of fluctuating enrollments, then by enrollment increases in the late 1980s. Enrollment declines early in the 1990s have been followed by recent upswings. These trends vary by college, program, and student type.

Figure 1.1 displays a long-range pattern of enrollment trends for nearly three decades at County Community College (County CC) in State A. Comparing its fall headcount enrollments with other community colleges in State A (Eastern Community College, Northern Community College, Western Community College, and Southern Community College) and with colleges across the country, it is evident that County CC appears to have recently had rather significant

losses, after experiencing the more typical enrollment pattern before the 1990s. However, closer inspection of the data and discussions with County CC's staff reveal that the college underwent a reorganization in 1993 in which a significant portion of its curriculum was changed from credit to noncredit. Because these restructured classes were then offered outside the regular curriculum, their enrollments were no longer counted in normal data reporting. Consequently, although enrollments at County CC appear to have declined substantially more than those at neighboring and comparable community colleges in its own state, adjusting for County CC's reorganization reveals that its enrollment losses were similar in magnitude and timing to losses at like institutions in the same state (though still sufficiently higher than patterns elsewhere in the country to be of concern to the staff at County CC). It is important to identify early in the analysis any changes in the way a college's enrollment data have been collected, organized, and

Figure 1.1 Fall Enrollment at County Community College, State A Community Colleges, and U.S. Community Colleges: 1960–1997

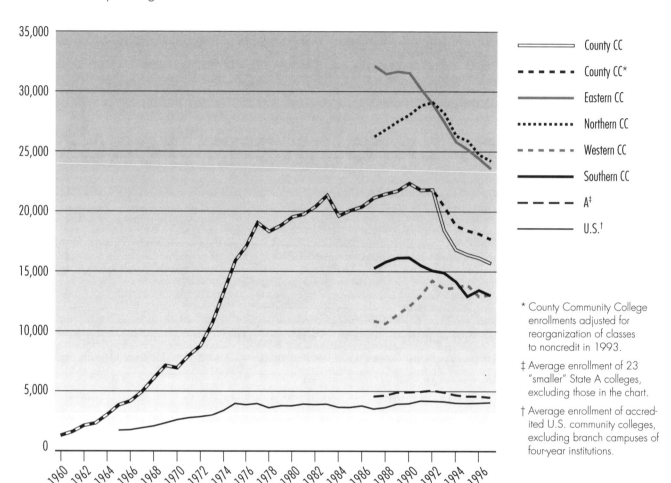

* County Community College enrollments adjusted for reorganization of classes to noncredit in 1993.

‡ Average enrollment of 23 "smaller" State A colleges, excluding those in the chart.

† Average enrollment of accredited U.S. community colleges, excluding branch campuses of four-year institutions.

reported in order to control for those changes throughout the work. Otherwise, conclusions will be invalid.

When overall trend periods have been established, the work proceeds with examining enrollment subsets. Metropolitan Community College (Metro CC) in State B (figure 1.2) has had four major periods of enrollment trends, which are reflected in similar ways for full-time and part-time students. By contrast, enrollment in Metro CC's once-flourishing noncredit program declined

in the late 1980s and has not yet recovered.

Even if extended time series data are not available, it is useful to continue the analysis of the components of a college's enrollment. For instance, enrollment at County Community College in the early 1990s declined equally among full- and part-time students (figure 1.3). The same pattern does not hold true if students are analyzed in terms of their program objectives: County CC's emphasis on occupational training has declined in relation to the number of current

Figure 1.2 Metro Community College Enrollment by Credit and Load: 1970–1997

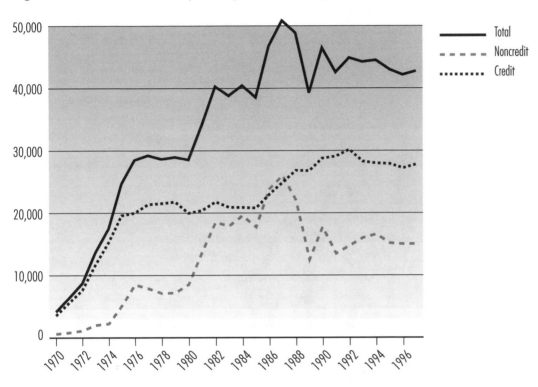

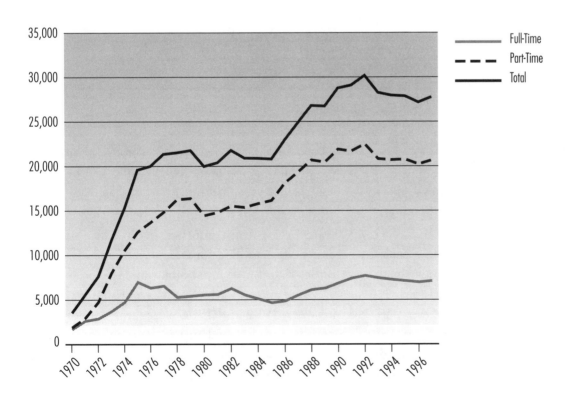

Figure 1.3 County Community College Enrollment by Load, Objective, and Residence: 1970–1997

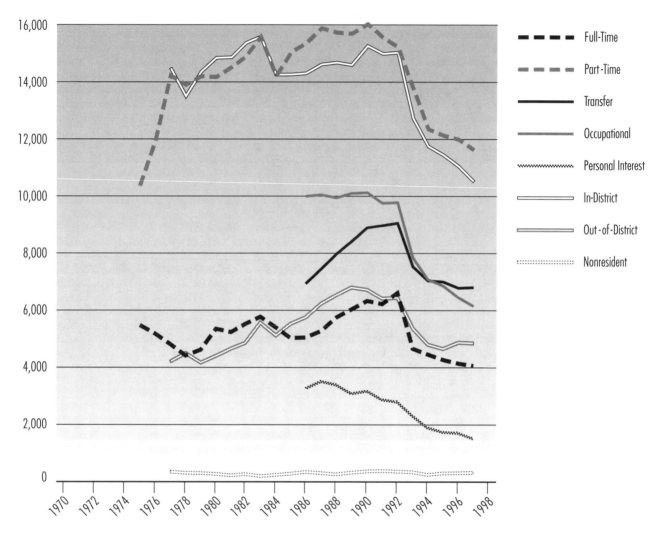

students who indicate they intend to transfer. Moreover, the 1990s enrollment declines at County CC have been primarily among residents of the college's district and far less so among students who live outside the district.

A college's enrollment trends are also revealed through student demographics, activities, backgrounds, and educational choices. Table 1.1 depicts data that can be used to begin this analysis.

Using the trend periods identified in this table, it is easy to see which students did or did not drive enrollments. Substantial enrollment

growth at Metro CC between 1985 and 1992 was largely among students who enrolled at Metro CC Campuses 1 and 2; minority females; continuing students, rather than those who were new or transferring from another institution; and students who enrolled for transfer or general studies, rather than for occupational training.

By contrast, Metro CC's enrollment losses between 1992 and 1996 were largely among students who attended in the evening, attended at Campus 1, enrolled for occupational training (transfer student counts increased), were Anglo (the number of minority students increased), and lived in Metro CC's geographic district.

Still other patterns emerge in Metro CC's enrollment reversal in fall 1997, which was concentrated almost solely among students who were new, and district residents at Campus 2.

After analyzing the factors causing these patterns, Metro CC forecasts its likely future enrollment mix and begins to formulate and simulate the consequences of the policies and strategies that are most likely to enable the college to achieve its educational goals and objectives. All of this is determined by first identifying the trends and patterns.

Table 1.1 Metro Community College Enrollment Trends by Student Type: 1985–1997

	Fall 1985	Fall 1992	% Chg.	Fall 1992	Fall 1996	% Chg.	Fall 1996	Fall 1997	% Chg.
Credit Headcount	20,801	30,175	45.1%	30,175	27,177	-9.9%	27,177	27,761	2.1%
Day	–	13,439	–	13,439	14,056	4.6%	14,056	14,522	3.3%
Evening	–	9,429	–	9,429	7,210	-23.5%	7,210	7,461	3.5%
Both	–	7,307	–	7,307	5,911	-19.1%	5,911	5,778	-2.3%
Full-Time	4,662	7,693	65.0%	7,693	6,961	-9.5%	6,961	7,101	2.0%
Part-Time	16,139	22,482	39.3%	22,482	20,216	-10.1%	20,216	20,660	2.2%
Male	9,894	13,622	37.7%	13,622	12,102	-11.2%	12,102	12,386	2.3%
Female	10,907	16,553	51.8%	16,553	15,075	-8.9%	15,075	15,375	2.0%
Native American	455	710	56.0%	710	925	30.3%	925	987	6.7%
African American	770	981	27.4%	981	1,060	8.1%	1,060	993	-6.3%
Asian American	574	938	63.4%	938	1,044	11.3%	1,044	1,100	5.4%
Hispanic	3,770	7,397	96.2%	7,397	7,513	1.6%	7,513	7,657	1.9%
Anglo/Other	15,232	20,062	31.7%	20,062	16,635	-17.1%	16,635	17,014	2.3%
New	4,342	5,127	18.1%	5,127	5,001	-2.5%	5,001	5,777	15.5%
Transfer	2,587	3,254	25.8%	3,254	2,864	-12.0%	2,864	2,425	-15.3%
Continuing	9,329	14,963	60.4%	14,963	13,370	-10.6%	13,370	13,244	-0.9%
Returning	4,543	6,831	50.4%	6,831	5,942	-13.0%	5,942	6,315	6.3%
District Residents	18,761	26,233	39.8%	26,233	23,323	-11.1%	23,323	24,002	2.9%
State Residents	838	2,155	157.2%	2,155	2,178	1.1%	2,178	1,959	-10.1%
U.S. Residents	759	1,045	37.7%	1,045	1,114	6.6%	1,114	1,193	7.1%
Foreign	443	742	67.5%	742	562	-24.3%	562	607	8.0%
H.S. Grads	–	23,109	–	23,109	20,424	-11.6%	20,424	–	–
GED Recipients	–	2,258	–	2,258	1,735	-23.2%	1,735	–	–
Non H.S. Grads	–	4,808	–	4,808	5,018	4.4%	5,018	–	–

– indicates data not available.

Table 1.1 (continued)

	Fall 1985	Fall 1992	% Chg.	Fall 1992	Fall 1996	% Chg.	Fall 1996	Fall 1997	% Chg.
Transfer	5,424	9,200	69.6%	9,200	10,615	15.4%	10,615	10,786	1.6%
Occupational	8,945	9,721	8.7%	9,721	7,683	-21.0%	7,683	7,924	3.1%
General Studies	4,432	8,254	86.2%	8,254	5,797	-29.8%	5,797	6,676	15.2%
Spec., Undecided	2,000	3,000	50.0%	3,000	3,082	2.7%	3,082	2,375	-22.9%
<20	3,366	5,297	57.4%	5,297	5,498	3.8%	5,498	5,676	3.2%
20-29	9,595	13,422	39.9%	13,422	12,251	-8.7%	12,251	12,335	0.7%
30-39	4,716	6,506	38.0%	6,506	4,998	-23.2%	4,998	4,912	-1.7%
40-49	1,996	3,563	78.5%	3,563	3,136	-12.0%	3,136	3,280	4.6%
50-59	722	958	32.7%	958	959	0.1%	959	1,141	19.0%
>59	275	262	-4.7%	262	261	-0.4%	261	315	20.7%
Campus 1	5,163	9,340	80.9%	9,340	5,853	-37.3%	5,853	5,703	-2.6%
Campus 2	537	1,638	205.0%	1,638	2,167	32.3%	2,167	2,487	14.8%
Campus 3	6,825	10,216	49.7%	10,216	9,759	-4.5%	9,759	9,836	0.8%
Campus 4	3,700	5,196	40.4%	5,196	4,800	-7.6%	4,800	4,813	0.3%
Campus 5	9,008	13,665	51.7%	13,665	12,752	-6.7%	12,752	12,655	-0.8%
Tech Center	493	853	73.0%	853	949	11.3%	–	–	–

– indicates data not available.

CHAPTER TWO

What Causes Important Enrollment Trends?

This chapter uses a statistical model and related reasoning to explain the trends identified in chapter 1. The impact on enrollment of factors like tuition and fees, budgets, population, and unemployment are analyzed, along with events that are unique to a particular college, such as curriculum reorganization, calendar change, and other major policy changes. This analysis makes thorough use of statistics that measure how well the model fits the empirical data.

The model is causal in that it explains community college enrollment as being dependent on a number of independent variables that operate simultaneously, just as they do in the real world. The model is run a number of times with different groupings of the independent variables to secure the most accurate picture of how enrollment is determined over the long term and during each of the college's unique trend periods.

The specific form of the ESP model is a linear regression. Its technical explanation, including model parameters and measures, appears in appendix B.

Long-Term Enrollment Fluctuation

To illustrate the process (figure 2.1), suppose the first run of the model on data for Rural Community College between 1966 and 1996 results in high predictive capability (close to actual estimates) and relatively low values for the model's error terms. The error terms are serially correlated (one year is similar to the next year or the prior year). The model overestimates Rural CC enrollment between 1966 and 1970, underestimates enrollment from 1971 to 1979, and overestimates enrollment between 1983 and 1992. This result suggests that the model lacks one or more factors important to enrollment. Discussions with Rural CC's staff reveal that these discrepancies are due largely to the impact of the college's curriculum, along with academic calendar and other changes in 1971 and 1983—factors not included in the first run. To correct this, a "policy" variable is added to the succeeding runs, which produce a far better fit of the data.

Returning to the example of County CC in

Figure 2.1a Model Run for Rural Community College Full-Time-Equivalent Enrollment, Actual and Estimated: 1966–1996

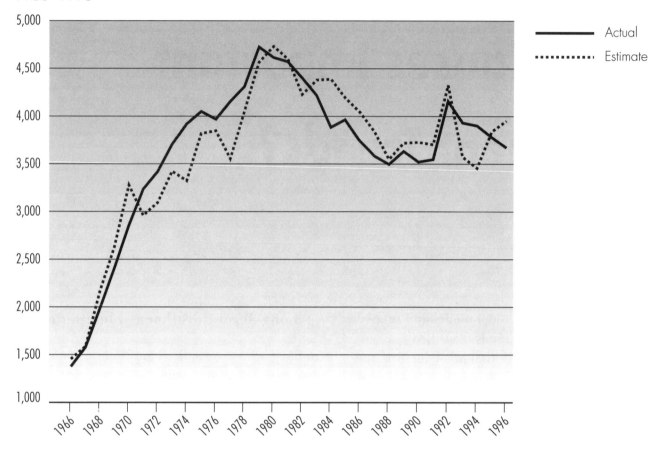

Figure 2.1b
Model Run for Rural
Community College
Full-Time-Equivalent
Enrollment, Model
Error: 1966–1996

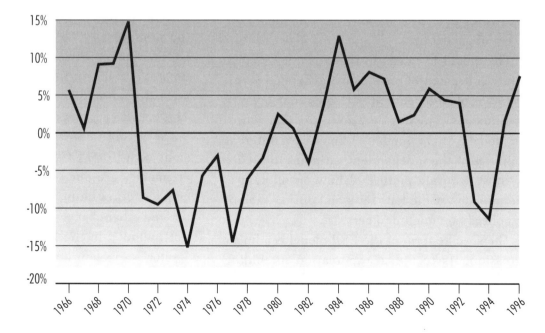

Table 2.1 Baseline Runs of ESP Model for County Community College

	Run A 1965–97	Run B 1976–97
Overall Model Estimate		
Coefficient of Determination (R^2)	0.984	0.913
F-Ratio (Significance of R^2)	392.2[†]	37.5[†]
Durbin Watson (DW) Statistic	1.24	2.53
Average Percent Error in Prediction	4.3%	4.8%
Elasticities of Independent Variables		
County CC Tuition and Fees	-0.30[‡]	-0.33[*]
State University Tuition and Fees	—	+0.36[*]
County CC Service Area Population	+1.70[‡]	+0.32
County CC Service Area Unemployment Rate	+0.18[†]	+0.13[*]
County CC Unrestricted General Budget	+0.67[†]	+0.33
Policy Variable[§]	-0.05[†]	-0.06[†]

See appendix A for technical explanation of results. *Significant at the $P<.05$ level. ‡Significant at the $P<.01$ level. †Significant at the $P<.001$ level. §Characterizing County CC actions in 1993–94.

table 2.1, the model provides an excellent fit—explanation of enrollment fluctuation—of the college's data between 1965 and 1997 (run A), which enables a number of observations to be made about the individual factors that determine enrollment. To begin looking at specific periods, the model is also run on data for 1976 to 1997 (run B).

First, the results for County CC's tuition and fees are what one might expect. This factor has a statistically significant and negative impact on County CC's enrollment: When tuition and fees increase, other things being equal, enrollment decreases. The tuition and fee elasticity of -0.3 indicates that for every 1 percent increase in real (price-adjusted) tuition and fees—about $1.65 per unit, or nearly $12 per term for the student carrying seven units at County Community College—there is a 0.3 percent decline in enrollment, other things being equal.

Although the effect is modest, increases in County CC's tuition and fees will reduce its enrollment, unless other factors intervene.

Also as expected, tuition and fees at nearby State University (SU) exert the opposite effect on County CC's enrollment. When they increase, students are more likely to enroll at County CC because it becomes less expensive than attending SU's lower division. This is demonstrated in table 2.1 by an SU fee elasticity of +0.36. This is important for County CC because it shows that County is a "close substitute" for SU's lower division. Students consider County CC to be an acceptable institution at which to begin postsecondary work, and they are confident that they will be able to transfer to SU to complete their baccalaureates.

Second, unemployment in County CC's service area has a significant and positive impact on enrollment: When unemployment increases, other

Table 2.2 Relative Impact of Variables in ESP Model

Variable	Elasticity	Average Annual Change (Absolute)	Resulting Enrollment Change (Absolute)	Impact "Share"
Manageable				
County CC Tuition and Fees	-0.33	4.4%	1.5%	0.23
County CC Budget	0.33	3.1%	1.0%	0.16
Unmanageable				
SU Tuition and Fees	0.36	4.1%	1.5%	0.24
Area Unemployment	0.13	15.4%	2.0%	0.32
Area Population	0.32	1.0%	0.3%	0.05

things being equal, enrollment increases. The recent effect of unemployment seems to have been less than it was during County CC's early history, however. This is important because it suggests that economic swings may have less impact on community college enrollment than they once did. There could be several reasons for this: students enroll to upgrade their skills whether or not they are employed, County CC's training programs are less relevant than they once were, or other institutions that offer programs similar to County's have increased their share of the market.

Third, two other factors that are thought to be important determinants of County CC's enrollment—operating budget and service area population—are both positively related to enrollment. Like unemployment, however, their significance appears to have declined somewhat in recent years.

A policy variable added to the analysis to "explain" the impact of County CC's 1993–94 actions proves to be important, as measured by its elasticity and statistical significance in table 2.1. Besides improving the overall fit of the model, this variable also results in the estimated values of the other variables being more accurate.

While elasticities with respect to County CC's enrollment from the model are useful in explaining the college's enrollment fluctuation, the relative impact of each variable can also be interpreted in the context of its own fluctuation. This is illustrated in table 2.2.

Thus, while the elasticity of the area unemployment rate, with respect to County CC's enrollment, is a modest 0.13, its fluctuation has been dramatic, averaging more than 15 percent annually. Therefore, its impact on County CC's enrollment has been at least as great as the impact of the next strongest determinants—tuition and fees at County CC and SU—which, in turn, have affected enrollment more than County's budget changes have. Area population has had the least impact on enrollment fluctuation.

The model works well partly because, with one exception, the independent variables are not highly interrelated. The exception is the correlation between population and County CC budget (r = +.860); they both tend to change in the same direction at the same time, and, as a result, may mask one another's influence on enrollment. Moreover, this relationship appears to differ before and after County CC's reorganization in 1993. One solution to this potential problem, which can distort model results, is simple: Use *market penetration* (enrollment divided by population [E/P]), rather than just enrollment, as the dependent variable. This not only solves the statistical problem but also provides a useful measure (E/P) that County CC can use for planning.

Short-Term Trend Periods

The above analysis, together with data on the college's major trends in chapter 1, provides the basis for observations about the character of and possible reasons for enrollment fluctuation during each of a college's major trend periods.

To continue the illustration with County CC's experience, it is possible to make the following observations, which have direct implications for planning and managing County CC:

♦ The period 1957 to 1977 at County CC was characterized by rapid enrollment growth (average annual increases of nearly 20 percent), marking County CC's early development and fueled in part by robust growth in the local area population.

♦ A later period, from 1984 to 1990, marked a time of renewed but moderate growth (+2 percent annually) in enrollment. According to data, County CC's service area unemployment decreased during most of this period, from 11 percent in 1984 to 7 percent in 1990, and the number of students seeking occupational training stabilized, although significant increases were reported among students who were employed and attending both day and evening classes. Enrollment by students who intended to transfer increased significantly.

♦ Specific large gains between 1984 and 1990 were reported for first-time County CC enrollees who had prior college experience, older students (40 to 60), and students from outside the college district.

Except for a 1988 increase, fees for in-district students were stable, on average, between 1984 and 1990. By contrast, fees for out-of-district students increased continuously. Yet, nondistrict students increased by nearly one-third, while in-district students increased by just 7 percent. Enrollment gains were supported by sizeable and consistent increases in County CC's budgets and services.

Continued analysis shows that during the most recent trend period, 1992 to 1997, County CC's enrollments declined significantly and continually, apparently to about 28 percent. But a large portion of the loss during this period—perhaps as many as 2,000 students—took place in 1993, when County CC's curriculum was reorganized from the regular college instructional program into a cost-recovery institute operation. If this estimate is accurate, the 1992 to 1997 enrollment loss at County CC is 21 percent, rather than 28 percent. The balance of the two years of largest losses (-1,400 headcount enrollment in 1992–93; -1,600 headcount enrollment in 1993–94) can be attributed in part to large decreases in area unemployment, from 8 percent in 1991 to 3 percent in 1997.

During the five-year period 1992 to 1997, the largest losses occurred among County CC's students who were

♦ middle-aged (30 to 50)

♦ white or African American

♦ reporting some prior college experience

♦ returning to County CC after stopping out

◆ transferring from another college

◆ seeking occupational training

By contrast, the fewest losses—even some increases—during 1992 to 1997 were among students who were

◆ new to County CC without prior college experience

◆ young (the number of those under 20 increased)

◆ Hispanic (their number increased)

◆ attending classes on (rather than off) the college's main campus

◆ receiving financial aid (the number increased by 2 percent)

These patterns of decreases and increases in student enrollment, together with their probable causes, can help County CC examine the portion of its service area population it serves—its market penetration—and assess alternative enrollment planning and management strategies, a topic revisited to in chapter 12.

What Is the Enrollment Behavior of Specific Groups of Students?

Results from the ESP analysis, together with identified trends, can indicate what factors are important in determining the enrollment of specific groups of students. These groups are categorized by such measures as residence (near to or far from the college), demographics (gender, age, race, ethnicity), and academic choices (load, program, time, location, and mode of attendance).

Student residence is of obvious importance as a community college prepares a marketing and public-information plan for its service areas, especially if patterns of enrollment and patterns of population differ by area. For example, County Community College serves two areas: an urban district where the population has stabilized and is predicted to decline in the future, and a suburban-rural outer area where population is expected to grow substantially, but where few other postsecondary institutions have a presence.

Using the model to compare behaviors of the urban, *district*, resident population and the suburban-rural, *nondistrict*, resident population reveals the following:

- Nondistrict residents have been more sensitive to County CC's tuition and fee changes and budget changes than have district residents.

- Nondistrict residents also react more to increases in SU's tuition and fees—by attending County CC—than do district residents.

- Both resident and nonresident enrollments at County CC are affected positively by changes in area unemployment rates, even though the rates in outlying areas have been more volatile.

As discussed in chapter 12, knowledge of these differences in likely student behavior provides County Community College with valuable information for planning its delivery and marketing strategies, as well as for curriculum and budget development.

The same basic model can be used to analyze student demographics and academic choices. For example, table 3.1 (page 19) shows the following for Metro Community College:

◆ Male enrollment at Metro CC increases when the area unemployment rate increases; female enrollment does not.

◆ Male and female enrollment increases as Metro's budget increases and campuses are added.

◆ Males are slightly more responsive than females to Metro's tuition and fee increases.

Applying the model to Metro CC's five major racial and ethnic categories of student enrollment shows the following:

◆ Tuition and fee increases have a negative impact on enrollment of Anglo, Native American, and African American students, but not on enrollment of Hispanic and Asian students.

◆ Economic downturns and increased unemployment induce the enrollment of Anglo and Hispanic students far more than they do the enrollment of other students.

◆ Budget increases by Metro CC lead to increases in enrollment for all racial and ethnic groups; adding campuses primarily affects Anglo and African American enrollment.

Academic Choices

It can also be seen from the results in table 3.1 that full-time enrollment at Metro CC is statisti-

cally determined (in a positive way) by the numbers of area high school graduates, by area unemployment, and by Metro's budget. It is not at all determined by Metro's tuition and fee changes, new Metro campus sites, or the local university's (U) tuition and fees. This suggests that students do not consider Metro to be a substitute for the local university; for example, it is not a place to begin studies, then transfer to complete studies for a baccalaureate degree. This warrants further analysis by Metro CC staff.

Students who enroll part time, by contrast, are sensitive to Metro CC's tuition and fees (elasticity [e] = -0.47) and to the addition of new campus sites. This is a typical finding at most community colleges. For part-timers, the price of college is a major consideration; they tend more often than full-timers to be financially independent, relying on their own earnings (rather than the earnings of parents or others), and few of them qualify for financial aid. But, they are less affected than full-timers by unemployment rates and by college budget increases.

Metro CC students' academic loads (the average number of units per student) increase as the college's budgets and tuition and fees increase (and part-time enrollment decreases); however, academic loads decrease as enrollment increases and as new campus sites are added, since these shifts involve relatively more part-time than full-time students.

Data show that the number of students who attend Metro only in the evening has declined substantially over the past decade. These students differ dramatically from day students in their reaction to the factors in the analysis. Evening students are sensitive to Metro's tuition and fee changes (e = -1.20), whereas students who attend during the day are not (e = +0.37). Evening enrollment increases with increases in the unemploy-

Table 3.1 Application of ESP Model to Enrollment Behavior of Metro Community College Students by Demographics and Academic Choices

by DEMOGRAPHICS							
	Gender		*Race and Ethnicity*				
	Male	**Female**	**African American**	**Asian**	**Hispanic**	**Native American**	**Anglo**
Equation							
R²	0.945	0.959	0.970	0.984	0.975	0.974	0.935
F-Ratio	**75.1**	**103.3**	**139.6**	**275.4**	**173.0**	**160.6**	**63.4**
DW Statistic	1.51	1.30	2.15	1.10	1.54	2.03	0.94
Average %-Off	5.6%	6.2%	5.0%	9.6%	6.9%	6.4%	6.5%
Enrollment - Elasticities							
MCC Tuition and Fees	-0.34	<u>-0.28</u>	<u>-0.21</u>	**0.90**	0.09	<u>-0.43</u>	<u>-0.47</u>
U Tuition and Fees	0.18	0.10	<u>-0.64</u>	-0.19	-0.09	<u>-0.74</u>	0.29
Area Population	-0.43	0.24	<u>-0.80</u>	<u>1.36</u>	-0.18	0.58	-0.08
Area Unemployment	**0.52**	0.19	<u>0.22</u>	0.04	**0.41**	-0.10	<u>0.36</u>
MCC Budget	**0.88**	**0.67**	**1.31**	<u>0.74</u>	**1.51**	**1.40**	<u>0.49</u>
MCC Campus Sites	<u>0.25</u>	<u>0.37</u>	**0.29**	-0.01	-0.18	-0.22	**0.49**

by ACADEMIC CHOICES							
	Time		*Academic Load*			*Program*	
	Day	**Evening**	**Full-Time**	**Part-Time**	**Units**	**Transfer**	**Occup.**	**General Studies**
Equation							
R²	0.988	0.858	0.927	0.958	0.819	0.978	0.925	0.923
F-Ratio	**344.0**	**27.1**	**55.7**	**98.8**	**20.6**	**191.5**	**54.5**	**52.9**
DW Statistic	1.35	1.34	2.00	0.98	1.72	2.19	1.70	**0.64**
Average %-Off	4.1%	9.4%	5.2%	6.7%	3.1%	6.9%	7.6%	10.3%
Enrollment - Elasticities							
MCC Tuition and Fees	**0.37**	**-1.20**	0.36	**-0.47**	<u>0.16</u>	-0.17	**-0.77**	-0.08
U Tuition and Fees	0.02	0.61	<u>-0.57</u>	0.38	<u>-0.41</u>	-0.22	0.20	0.24
Area Population	<u>0.55</u>	-0.20	<u>1.17</u>	0.32	<u>-0.44</u>	0.14	-0.69	0.81
Area Unemployment	**0.26**	<u>0.59</u>	**0.69**	<u>0.28</u>	0.10	<u>0.23</u>	**0.50**	0.23
MCC Budget	**0.74**	<u>0.61</u>	**0.97**	<u>0.48</u>	**0.45**	**1.44**	<u>0.61</u>	0.25
MCC Campus Sites	<u>0.16</u>	<u>0.48</u>	**-0.43**	**0.45**	<u>-0.23</u>	<u>-0.21</u>	**0.67**	0.11

Note: **Bold face** = significant at P < 0.01. <u>Underlined</u> = significant at P < 0.10

ment rate and with the addition of new campus sites. Day students exhibit similar responses, but to a lesser degree. During the 1980s and 1990s Metro's budget increases appear to have had a greater positive impact on day enrollment than on evening enrollment.

The number of students attending Metro for occupational preparation has also declined substantially over the past decade. For the first time ever at Metro CC, in 1993 more students enrolled for transfer than for job training.

Occupational enrollments are far more sensitive to Metro's tuition and fee changes (e = -0.77), new campus sites (e = +0.67), and changes in the area's unemployment rate (e = +0.50) than are transfer enrollments (e = -0.17, -0.21, and +0.23,

respectively). However, it appears that increases in Metro's budget have led to more transfer enrollments than occupational enrollments.

These findings have led Metro CC to reconsider its curriculum, marketing, and overall support of evening occupational programs, and to attempt a reconstruction of these programs, an important part of its mission.

Further insights about the behavior of specific groups of students may be gained by comparing the enrollment trends shown in table 1.1 (page 9) to findings about their causes shown in table 3.1. After the impact of factors that are within and outside of a college's control are considered (chapters 4 and 5), the full picture of the college's enrollment patterns begins to emerge.

How Do Factors within the College's Control Affect Enrollment?

This chapter examines how enrollment is affected by factors that are within a college's control, including tuition and fees, curriculum, delivery style, and market and management initiatives.

If these factors do affect enrollment, they are powerful tools that the college can use to plan and determine its future course. Results of the econometric model displayed in table 3.1 for Metro Community College provide an excellent illustration of this approach.

Tuition and Fees

The -0.3 to -0.8 range of elasticities (e) shown in table 3.1 that result from various runs of Metro CC's tuition and fees (in relation to enrollment), while significant in nearly all cases, would have to be considered moderate in their impact on enrollment. Metro CC's tuition and fee elasticities are similar to values found at Urban Community College, also in State B (e = -0.4), but somewhat lower than findings from studies of community college students in State D (e = -0.7 to -1.2), and lower than values found in a review of two-year college studies by Brinkman and Leslie (1987), in which national student price-response data reveal a fee elasticity for community college students of about -0.9.

As table 3.1 shows, Metro CC's tuition and fees have the greatest impact on students who are Anglo (e = -0.47), Native American (e = -0.43), male (e = -0.34), attending part time (e = -0.47), attending in the evening (e = -1.20), and attending for occupational training (e = -0.77).

This analysis uses real (price-adjusted) tuition and fees, rather than nominal ones, an important distinction. The apparently large tuition and fee increases at Metro CC during the period 1970 to 1997 look modest when compared with changes in the prices of other goods and services in Metro's service area. The local consumer price

Figure 4.1 Metro Community College Price-Adjusted Budget, Fees, and Financial Aid per FTE Student: 1970–1996

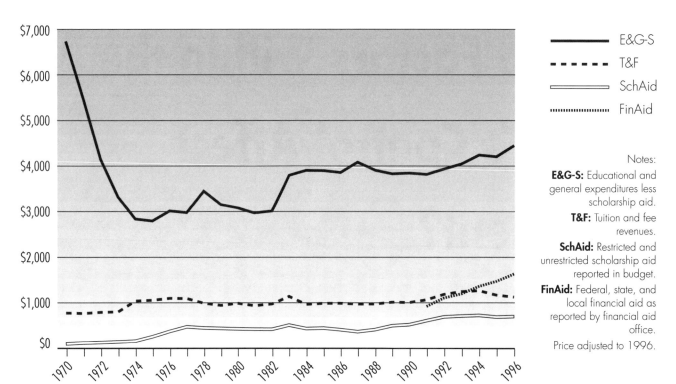

Notes:

E&G-S: Educational and general expenditures less scholarship aid.

T&F: Tuition and fee revenues.

SchAid: Restricted and unrestricted scholarship aid reported in budget.

FinAid: Federal, state, and local financial aid as reported by financial aid office.

Price adjusted to 1996.

index increased 6.2 percent. Although tuition and fees increased by 7.6 percent in that period, the price-adjusted increase amounts to 1.4 percent.

Colleges should anticipate local price changes when analyzing the implications of possible tuition and fee changes. Stable rates for Metro CC's tuition and fees during 1994, 1995, and 1996 meant that the cost of attendance declined by 2 percent or more each year, relative to the price of other goods and services.

The specification of student tuition and fees is typically the posted or published rates for tuition and registration. These charges usually represent more than 90 percent of all fees collected. Alternative specifications, such as revenue collected—incorporating miscellaneous campus fees, waivers, and noncollections—often produce statistically insignificant results. While it would be

useful to adjust for financial aid, data are usually not available to do so. No attempt is made to measure other direct costs (childcare, transportation, books, and supplies) or indirect costs (foregone earnings). Besides lacking data, these categories are not useful for policymaking since they are outside the college's control and difficult to predict.

Another exercise that is sometimes useful is to review changes over time in the share of a college's budget represented by tuition and fees. For instance, at Metro CC the share of operating budget outlays supported by student tuition and fee revenues declined from one-third in 1980 to one-fourth in 1996 (figure 4.1). Annual price-adjusted outlays per full-time-equivalent (FTE) student increased by half, from $3,000 to $4,500, while price-adjusted tuition and fee revenue per FTE student remained relatively constant at just over

$1,000. Student aid, measured by scholarship outlays in Metro CC's budget, increased slightly more than general revenues during the same period. These observations are quite important in some policy contexts.

Budget

Ideally, the concept of supply in the model would track the impact on enrollment of adding course sections, using new or different ways of delivery such as distance education, and supporting efforts such as student services and marketing. Because data for these measures are usually lacking, unrestricted college general operating budget outlays are often used as a proxy. Like tuition and fees, budget data are adjusted for price or cost-of-living adjustments (COLA) in order to measure their real impact on enrollment.

Questions about causation are inherent in econometric models of this kind: Does the model measure demand, supply, or both? Is there "simultaneous equation bias" in the use of one equation? Is enrollment driving budget, rather than budget driving enrollment, as is assumed in the model? Or does the impact of budget on enrollment lag by one year?

Results for Metro CC show a significant overall positive relationship between budget and enrollment, ranging from $e = +0.6$ to $e = +1.0$. Most likely, budget both promotes and responds to enrollment. This relationship is largest for Hispanic ($e = +1.51$), transfer ($e = +1.44$), Native American ($e = +1.40$), African American ($e = +1.31$), full-time ($e = +0.97$), male ($e = +0.88$), and day ($e = +0.74$) students.

Lagging enrollment rates (E/P) one year behind changes in Metro CC's budget reduces the measured relationship slightly, from $e = +0.70$ to $e = +0.45$. Eliminating budget from the model entirely reduces the model's overall explanatory power substantially.

It can be argued that, in many cases, a college's budget is largely outside its control. However, the way the budget is allocated—COLAs, infrastructure, and program improvements—is clearly within its control.

Campus Sites

The other supply element for which data are often available, major campus and outreach sites, produces statistically significant results for Metro CC enrollment:

$e = +0.2$ to $+0.3$ for enrollment (E)
$e = +0.1$ to $+0.2$ for college-going rate (E/P)

A new major site in an underserved portion of Metro's service area may be added to the existing six sites. If the past impact of new sites as measured in the analysis continues, this new site will add 2 to 3 percent to Metro's enrollment, or more than 500 new students, during its site's first year, apart from other factors. This initial impact will expand if and when the campus is developed.

The magnitude of the impact that factors under a college's control have on enrollment becomes critical as the college simulates different plans and initiatives, a topic considered in part 2.

CHAPTER FIVE

How Do Factors outside the College's Control Affect Enrollment?

This chapter examines factors that are outside a community college's control but that are known to affect enrollments. The empirical impact of these factors should be determined so the college may predict their future values in order to forecast and simulate enrollments. Factors outside the college's control include student financial aid, public policy, area demographic and economic conditions, and a number of other trends and events. The analysis cannot and need not address all of them.

Student Financial Aid

Student financial aid is considered to be an external variable because its determination is largely outside the college's control. At Metro CC, for example, 97 percent of student financial aid comes from federal grants, primarily Pell grants. At most colleges, state agencies and the college itself also provide some nominal aid.

Continuing with the illustration of Metro CC, federal aid grants doubled between 1991 and 1996. Decreasing state financial aid was more than replaced by Metro's own scholarship funds. Like most community colleges, Metro CC has no aid data available for the period before 1991, and incomplete reports for scholarship aid in Metro's budget are not sufficient for use in the ESP (figure 4.1). Lacking other data, the 1992 to 1996 impact of aid on enrollment appears problematic, since aid increased at 10 percent annually (in real terms) while enrollment declined by 3 percent annually.

Other survey data may be useful. At County CC, for example, although 8 out of 10 students work (4 full time, 4 part time), 1 out of 10 is seeking work, and 1 out of 10 is neither working nor seeking work, only 2 out of 10 students receive financial aid. Because it is likely that more students than this are eligible for aid, one of County CC's first steps would be to review its mechanism for determining student financial aid eligibility. Staff would need to assess possible improvements to this mechanism for their impact on the number and kind of additional students likely to enroll.

Policies and Practices of Other Providers

Changes in student tuition and fees at accessible four-year institutions are important to community college enrollment, since community college transfer programs often serve as a substitute for the lower division in those institutions. Also important are student charges at "close substitutes"—institutions that offer programs similar to those in community colleges. The University of Phoenix, for example, offers programs in health, business, computer science, and education that parallel those offered in many community colleges.

If enrollment at a community college is positively related to tuition and fees at the four-year institutions that are that college's close substitutes, the community college's enrollment will increase when the four-year institution's tuition and fees increase. This must be taken into account in forecasting enrollments at the community college.

Findings for County CC show that its enrollment increases as the nearby State University's tuition and fees increase and County becomes relatively more affordable, other things being equal. These elasticities are significant and high (+0.4 to +0.7) for both full- and part-time students at County CC, and especially for those who attend County CC from outside its geographic district (+1.0). By contrast, Metro CC does not show the same results with regard to the nearby University, which is of concern to Metro.

Also important for community college enrollments are changes in lower-division and transfer admissions policy and concurrent enrollments by community college students at four-year institutions.

Metro CC reports concurrent enrollments by more than 2,000 University students, who make up 8 percent of Metro's credit enrollment each term. These students typically attend full time, taking 10 units at the University and five at the community college. Their numbers were stable throughout the 1992–1996 period, although course enrollments increased in math, Spanish, and physical science and decreased in English. Concurrent enrollments will be affected by changes to the University's admissions requirements and must be a key component of Metro's enrollment planning.

The issue of other providers, such as proprietary institutions, although important for community college enrollment forecasting, is difficult to assess for at least two reasons. First, information is not available on the extent of their presence—physically or electronically—in a college's service area. Second, a college's offerings must be known, as well as relevant, to be competitive. There is evidence from a recent marketing study by County CC, for instance, that its computer science program is not as well known as it should be and that County's occupational programs are not well known among area employers. If so, this would affect County CC's enrollment.

Service Area Population

Ordinarily, a community college's enrollment tracks as a function of its service area demographics, although this empirical relationship can sometimes be problematic, as is seen in the continuing illustrations.

As expected, the number of high school graduates in Metro CC's service area is a significant determinant of Metro's full-time day enrollment (table 3.1, page 19). But, unexpectedly, total service area population is not a robust driver of total enrollment. Moreover, population is highly correlated on Metro CC's budget (simple correlation [r] = +0.97) and only when Metro's budget is removed from the model does population become significant and positive in determining overall enrollment. Consequently, most observations and the suggested forecasting model for a college such as Metro are based on using the participation rate (E/P) as the dependent variable, thereby eliminating population as a troublesome independent variable. Of course, future population must be projected in order to convert E/P to enrollment.

By contrast, service area population is positively related (as expected) to enrollment in the case of County CC, although its impact was stronger during earlier years than more recently. A high correlation of population and budget would lead to the recommendation that County CC's forecasting model use the participation rate as the dependent variable, as in the case of Metro CC.

Service Area Unemployment

Traditional and popular wisdom states that when economic conditions worsen and unemployment increases, individuals will enroll at or return to community colleges seeking training that will enable them to obtain employment again.

It is evident that changing area economic conditions have a consistent and positive impact on Metro CC's enrollment: Measured elasticities for the area unemployment rate range from +0.3 to +0.7. When the economy slows and unemploy-

ment increases, Metro's enrollment increases (table 3.1). Unemployment has the greatest impact on Metro's students who are male (e = +0.52), Hispanic (e = +0.41), enrolled full time (e = +0.69), enrolled only in the evening (e = +0.59), and enrolled for occupational training (e = +0.50). Despite some unusual fluctuations in Metro's area unemployment data, specifying unemployment rate is useful in both explaining and forecasting enrollment.

Questions have been raised about the traditional relationship between unemployment and community college enrollment. For example, it may appear that at County CC there is no direct link between the district employment/unemployment rates and headcount, as some colleges report. If true, this could suggest that, especially for those wanting to change careers or upgrade job skills, County CC's occupational education curriculum may be less relevant than it once was and is not, therefore, attractive to the unemployed. This also could mean that County's offerings are no longer competitive with the offerings of other providers, such as University of Phoenix and DeVry Institute, or the increasing number of institutions that provide courses over the Internet.

Closer analysis of the data actually supports the traditional assumption for County CC: low unemployment rates indicate lower community college enrollment. Economic conditions continue to affect County CC's enrollment, although less than in previous years. Measured elasticities of enrollment range from +0.1 to +0.3.

What Is the College's Market Penetration?

This section examines the college's market penetration (enrollment divided by population, or E/P): how it has changed over time (for subcategories of students as well as total enrollment); what factors drive it; and how it compares to other colleges locally, regionally, and nationally.

A specific answer to the question of market penetration for any community college depends on how the college's service area is defined and how the population of that service area is measured.

Defining the College's Service Area

Service area definition depends upon public policy, geography, and community culture. Thus, many different configurations are possible. County CC in State A, for instance, operates from a "district" tax base, organized around most of the secondary school districts in three contiguous counties. But County CC also serves individuals who live outside this area in the three nearby counties and in three other, outlying, counties. The population in the outlying area pays no local property taxes to support County CC, but its non-resident students pay more tuition than do district residents to attend County CC.

By contrast, Metro CC in State B serves primarily the county in which it is located, while adjacent counties are served by other community colleges. City CC, in State C, serves a major metropolitan area that overlaps the service areas of two other community colleges. In this case, as in many others, the colleges' service areas do not conform to the areas described by legal district boundaries.

In one sense, a community college's service area is whatever the college says it is, within the bounds of legal and organizational propriety. The key is that the college's claimed constituent community agrees and that other postsecondary institutions are aware of and, to some degree, acknowledge this definition.

Measuring Population

The other condition necessary for analyzing a college's market penetration is that the population of the college's service area can be measured consistently and accurately. Ideally, since the community college serves mostly an adult population (over 18), that cohort within the service area would be the desired measure. It is preferable to have forecast future, as well as historic, numbers.

Unfortunately, this is not always possible; sometimes planners will need to use total population numbers (including those under 18), because that measure is nearly always available.

To be most useful, the market penetration analysis should segment the college's enrollment for different groups of students by race and ethnicity, gender, age, and socioeconomic status.

Market Penetration over Time

To illustrate the process, research shows that Metro Community College achieved a rather high level of market penetration—as measured by fall

Figure 6.1 Metro and Comparative Community Colleges Fall Credit Enrollment per 1,000 Population: 1970–1997

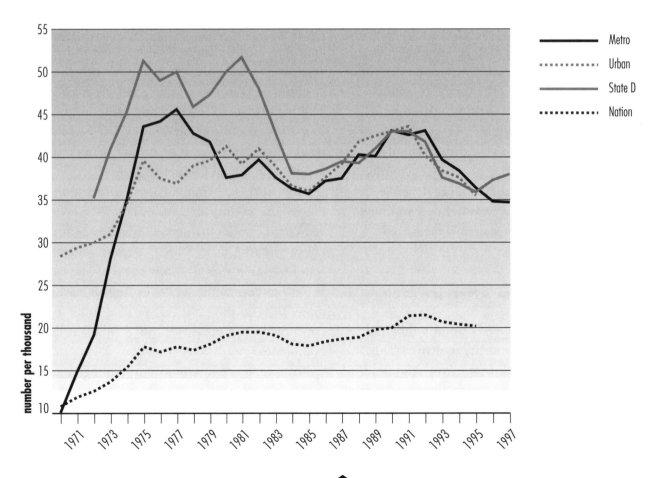

credit enrollment divided by total service area population—soon after its founding in 1970 (figure 6.1). By 1977, Metro's enrollment performance was quite favorable compared with that of a similar community college, Urban Community College, also in State B. It was also favorable to the experience of community colleges in adjacent State D, all of which boast much higher rates of market penetration or access than community colleges across the nation. Since 1977, however, Metro's performance has been uneven—as has been true elsewhere—and it has dropped significantly since 1992. And, while there is evidence that some other community colleges have started to rebuild their access, Metro seems to have stabilized and needs to review its position in this regard.

Using a different measure, full-year enrollment divided by population, Rural CC, in State C, had a peak in its access by 1979, slightly later than Metro's, followed by a substantial drop, another peak in 1995, and another drop (figure 6.2). Moreover, the market penetration at Rural has at times run counter to that of other community colleges in its own state. Rural CC needs to determine (1) if the data peaks, or spikes, in 1970 and 1979 are valid or are the result of measurement problems; (2) what changes to policy and practice produced the substantial decline in access between 1979 and 1985; and (3) whether

Figure 6.2 Rural and Other State C Colleges Full-Year Enrollment per 1,000 Population: 1965–1996

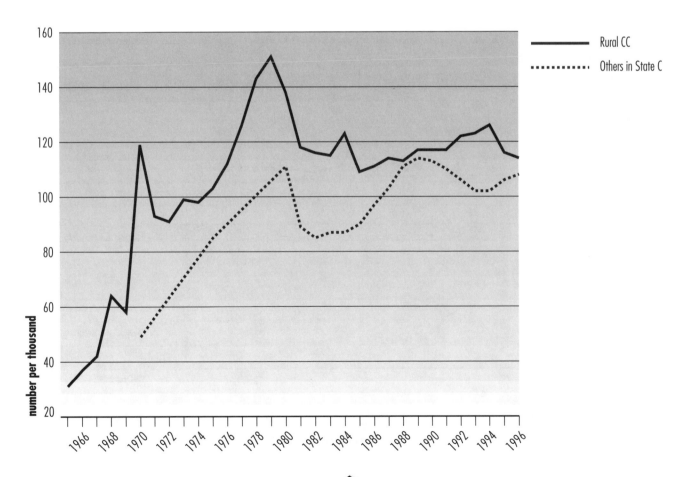

Rural CC's recent downturn in access can be expected to continue, and, if so, what steps can or should be taken to reverse it.

Comparative Market Penetration

Comparison with like community colleges can be difficult, especially if the college in question has an ambiguous service area. Using the complex organization of County CC illustrates this point. As expected, County CC's market penetration in its outlying, nondistrict, areas is less than that of its urban, district, area; but market penetration in the outlying area seems to have stabilized,

whereas market penetration in the urban area continues to decline (figure 6.3). The significance is that (1) outlying population is expected to grow more rapidly, and (2) County CC needs to determine why its access to populations near the college is declining.

In an effort to determine its overall market penetration relative to other similar colleges, County Community College compares its performance to its neighboring community colleges—Southeast, Southwest, and Border to like-sized urban colleges—Urban 1, Urban 2, Urban 3, Urban 4, and Urban 5; and to all other colleges in State A. These comparisons are difficult because of the varying specifications of County CC's ser-

Figure 6.3 County Community College Fall Enrollment per 1,000 Population by Residence: 1960–1997

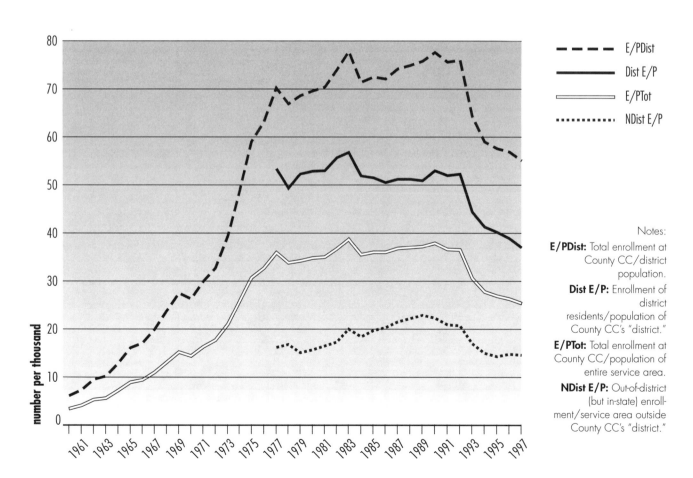

Notes:

E/PDist: Total enrollment at County CC/district population.

Dist E/P: Enrollment of district residents/population of County CC's "district."

E/PTot: Total enrollment at County CC/population of entire service area.

NDist E/P: Out-of-district (but in-state) enrollment/service area outside County CC's "district."

vice area. So, using three different definitions for County CC, it appears in figure 6.4 that, despite its concerns about recent trends, its market penetration compares favorably with the market penetration of colleges throughout the state. Even including some outlying areas that are not officially in its district, County CC's current market penetration equals that of its neighboring colleges, exceeds that of "like" colleges in its state, and substantially exceeds that of all other community colleges in State A. Narrower definitions of County CC's service area show its performance to be even more favorable.

The difficulty of measuring market penetration where service areas may overlap can be illus-

trated by the case of City CC, in a heavily populated metropolitan area of State C. City CC serves residents of five urban counties, with its highest market penetration in counties c, d, and e, where City CC's major campuses are located (figure 6.5). City CC's responsibilities for access in county d, however, are shared with the much smaller Outlying Community College. And, in two other counties, b and f, City CC shares its access responsibility with still other community colleges. Besides the complexity of maintaining consistent and accurate data and planning collaboratively with Outlying CC and other colleges, it appears that City CC would want to focus attention on its relatively low rates of market penetration in coun-

Figure 6.4 Fall Enrollment per 1,000 Service Area Population at State A Community Colleges: 1997

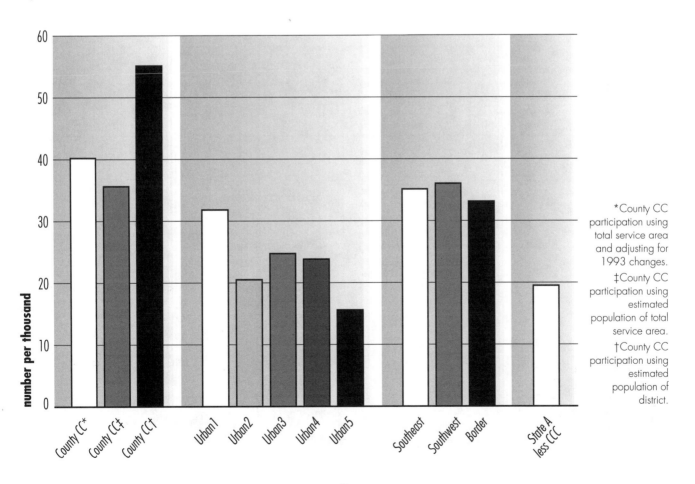

*County CC participation using total service area and adjusting for 1993 changes.
‡County CC participation using estimated population of total service area.
†County CC participation using estimated population of district.

ties c and e. Besides its role in county d, Outlying CC must determine its role, along with City CC and other colleges, in county b. The analysis of market penetration facing Rural CC, by contrast, appears far more simple: It essentially serves only county a, and quite well at that.

Market Penetration for Key Population Subgroups

To ensure that its access is broad and reasonably equitable across its service area, a college should examine market penetration for specific subgroups by age, gender, race and ethnicity, and socioeconomic and cultural status, among other categories. At this point in the analysis, data for either the college's student enrollment or its service area population tend to be limited. The work should proceed, however, since it provides necessary information for planning and marketing.

Concerned about its recent decline in market penetration, County CC reviewed the demographics of its enrollment and found that its greatest enrollment loss in recent years was among those aged 40 to 59 in its service area; the smallest loss was among those aged 18 and 19 (figure 6.6). In fact, County CC's 1995 market penetration for 18- to 19-year-olds exceeds the level recorded for them in 1980. The E/P for all other age groups has declined since 1980.

Using the same service area measure of popu-

Figure 6.5 Enrollment at State C Community Colleges per 1,000 County Population: 1996–97

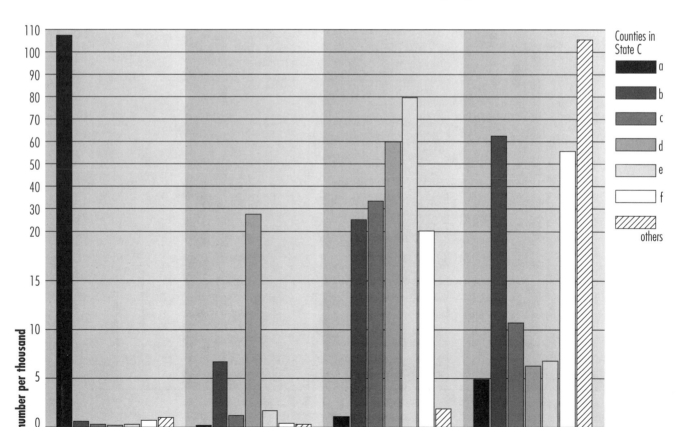

lation, County CC's market penetration for African Americans (41 enrollments per 1,000 population) was the lowest among the major racial and ethnic groups in 1992. Since that time this rate has declined by one-fifth, while, by contrast, the rate for whites has declined by one-third. Consequently, the rate for both groups is currently the same, 32 per 1,000. Taken together, other minority groups enroll in County CC at a higher rate, but it is not possible to distinguish the rate among Native American, Asian American, and Hispanic populations.

Another important target group for community colleges is recent high school graduates. This is because their level of market penetration is higher than that of any other specific student subgroup at the typical community college, and because in most communities members of the baby boom "echo" have started to emerge from high school; the number of high school graduates will continue to increase well into the next decade. (Figure 6.7 shows this trend at County CC in State A.)

To determine its market penetration or college-going rates of high school graduates across its service area, County CC collects data from each of its high schools. It groups these data for three areas: the "district" or urban area surrounding the main campus, outer "out-of-district" areas, and more distant "outer three county" areas.

Figure 6.6 County Community College Fall Enrollment per 1,000 Area Population by Age, Gender, and Race and Ethnicity

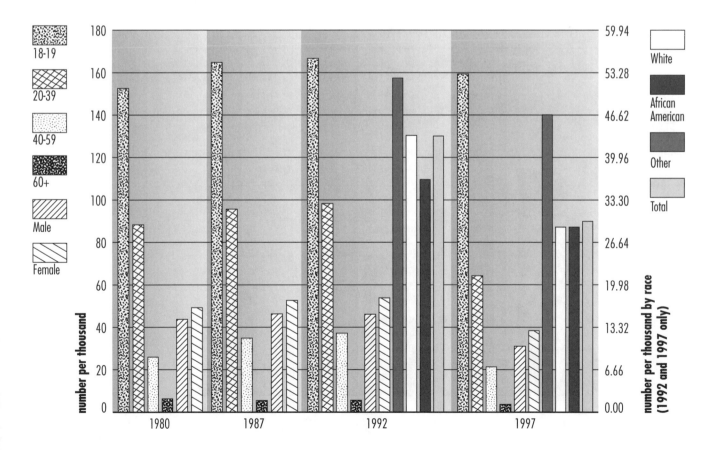

County CC finds significant differences in the enrollment rates of high school graduates (figure 6.8). These differences relate largely to high schools' distance from the main campus, but in two cases, counties j and m, surprisingly low rates require further analysis. County CC's marketing initiative with local area high schools benefits from the results of this analysis.

Figure 6.7 High School Graduates, County Community College, and Inner and Outer Service Areas, State A: Actual 1975–1997, Estimated 1998–2012

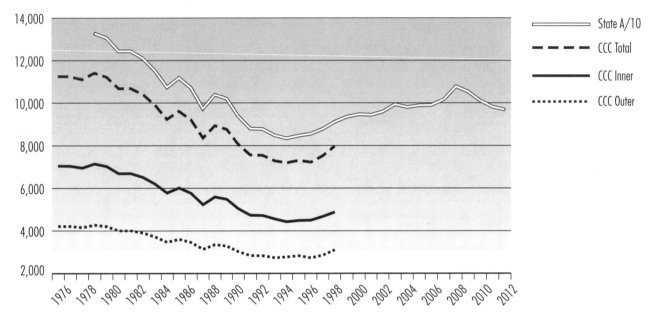

Figure 6.8 County Community College Enrollment Rates for Area High School Graduates: 1997

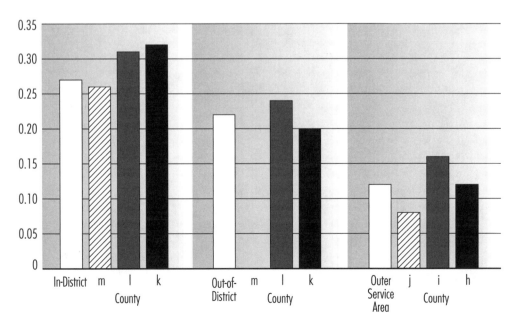

CHAPTER SEVEN

What Should the College's Market Penetration Be?

The answer to this question is developed by reference to what a community college has done, wants to do, and should do, based on its mission and the factors of technological change and educational opportunity or access. This chapter presents a process for developing explicit policy in this subjective area.

Several factors account for changes in the degree of market share or penetration a college has. An increasing number of high school graduates and a possible slowing of the economy, beginning in 1999 in most communities, would, other things being equal, result in increased market penetration at most community colleges.

Still other factors suggest that there should be increased participation at most community colleges (McIntyre 1997a) in technology, opportunity, and mission.

Because of technological change, job skill needs in most communities continue to rise at a significant rate (Kerr et al. 1994). Thus, other things (like the relative market share of other suppliers) being equal, community colleges should be increasing their level of service to those in their service areas by at least the same rate as the increase in needed postsecondary-level job skills. And, community colleges in most states provide educational opportunities to the disadvantaged in order to, among other things, reduce wage inequality (Lin and Vogt 1996). Moreover, a college has the responsibility of providing equal access to individuals throughout its service area. Finally, increased participation should follow from the ever-expanding mission of community colleges resulting from welfare reform and continued immigration, among other events.

Emerging information technology ensures that all core lower-division and many specialized occupational courses are available in the service area of most community colleges. Many community colleges themselves offer degrees, programs, and courses in a variety of disciplines over the Internet. But not all potential students will be able to access such courses, because of economic and other disadvantages. If such clients are not served by other providers, community colleges have the responsibility to make educational technology accessible to them.

Will community colleges be able to enhance their work in televised courses and in virtual colleges? Will they be able to partner with and broker instructional materials from competitors, growing enrollments with them rather than losing enrollments to them? Work by County Community College with nearby State University on a trucking management program illustrates a partnership in the virtual instruction realm.

An explicit community college policy on market penetration could separate the issue into three parts:

◆ To what extent should the college make up the (typical) decline in market penetration of the recent decade? Goals to restore market penetration levels should probably distinguish credit from noncredit objectives, with explicit recognition of contract and other "nonregular" instructional organization, and distinguish results of conscious policies from results due to likely external trends.

◆ Apart from restoration, the college may want to set goals for ongoing future changes in market penetration because of the changing factors of technology, opportunity, and mission.

◆ A college such as County CC should identify explicit policy on possible changes to its service area, and on how to penetrate new markets in outlying areas through new delivery sites or electronically.

The third part raises further questions: Will this effort require consideration of changing a college's organization, taxing authority, student tuition, and other policies? Can these changes include strategic partnerships with other postsecondary institutions or local business and industry?

Answers to these and related questions should provide a community college with more than enough information to make informed decisions about future goals for its level of access or market penetration.

Part 2
Forecasting, Simulating, and Planning

CHAPTER EIGHT

What Is a Useful Forecasting and Simulation Model?

The work in part 1 can be recast and used to forecast and simulate future enrollments. This chapter covers theoretical and practical considerations, including what problems to look for and how to deal with incomplete or possibly invalid data, and uses illustrations from the author's recent experience to demonstrate points.

Work at a number of community colleges suggests the merit of a two-step enrollment simulation and planning (ESP) process where a college's future market penetration or participation rate—enrollment divided by population (E/P)—is estimated using a causal regression model like that used to explain enrollment fluctuation in part 1. This estimate is then applied to projections of the college's service area population in order to forecast future enrollment. (The specific form of this model is described in appendix C.)

Validation

Use of this causal model relies on affirmative answers to three key questions:

- Are the model's independent variables related to enrollment?

- Are these relationships stable and predictable?

- Can the independent variables be forecast reliably?

The study's explanation phase in part 1 answers the first two questions. The third question is more difficult to answer. Forecasts of college enrollment often err because of faulty projections of independent variables describing an area's economy or the college's budget. The best solution to this problem may be to use a range of plausible scenarios about the future of a college's service area, arrived at by consensus of college staff or other experts. Assumptions used for each scenario can be examined for their likelihood, and model output can then be considered for its planning implications.

This proposed two-step forecasting process should be simple, straightforward, robust, and informative.

Easy simulations enable staff to examine the specific consequences of using a wide variety of policy and trend packages.

The model is straightforward. Use of enrollment divided by population eliminates the problem, for example, that County CC budget and population are historically correlated. Other independent variables are only moderately correlated.

The model is usually robust statistically, displaying a high overall fit and modest residual errors, indicating that nothing of consistent importance is omitted. Independent variables are typically statistically significant and strongly related to E/P, the dependent variable.

Use of E/P is also informative for college planning and decision making because it separates the college's actual and desired market penetration—a policy issue—from the externally determined population demographics of the college's service areas. Derivation of full-time-equivalent (FTE) from enrollment, in a possible third step, would allow college staff to separately analyze and forecast changes in student academic loading and curriculum and changes in delivery time and location, as well as to simulate future budgets.

The process is simple because the 10 input variables required by the model are accessible and the model software is easy to run. Every community college maintains data for five variables:

tuition and fees, budget, delivery strategies, enrollment, and FTE. The other variables (tuition and fees of other providers, area unemployment and population, index of government purchases or other appropriate index of community college costs, and local consumer price index) also are readily obtained and, to the degree necessary, valid. Moreover, the model, including the necessary statistical formulations and useful output graphics, can be programmed easily into a spreadsheet program.

Test Scenarios

The ESP model is validated and used as it is applied to several test or different future scenarios with different college enrollment outcomes described and analyzed.

Scenarios may be constructed in several ways, beginning with some degree of environmental scanning or futures research to develop a range of descriptions about the college's likely future. External information can be gathered from a variety of sources: newspapers, journals, books, periodicals, professional society publications, public agencies, private firms, and foundations. This information is increasingly available through Internet search engines, CD-ROMs, and other electronic tools; indeed, much of the demographic and economic information a college needs can be found on the Web.

Once gathered, information and data from these scans are analyzed to identify trends and possible future events pertinent to the college. To save time, the effort can focus primarily on the data elements needed for ESP:

- populations

- employment and unemployment rates

- state and local government purchase indexes

- consumer price index

- tuition and fees at "close substitute" institutions

- other general conditions

Numerous analytical techniques are available for this scanning (McIntyre 1997b). The next step in preparing for enrollment forecasts and simulations is for college staff to pose, narrow down, and agree upon a manageable set of preferred future policies and practices; this enables the other variables required by ESP to be specified:

- college tuition and fees

- college budget

- college delivery techniques

If there is not already a plan that specifies such future values, there are many group consensus-building techniques that can be used to arrive at one. These techniques differ in how they equalize input from each member, measure consensus, allot time, and intensify effort.

The results of the above efforts are then used to specify and run the ESP model and to analyze its results.

Figure 8.1 County Community College Budget, Tuition and Fees, Unemployment, and State University Tuition and Fees: Actual 1975–1997, Assumed 1998–2020, Ratios to 1975 Values

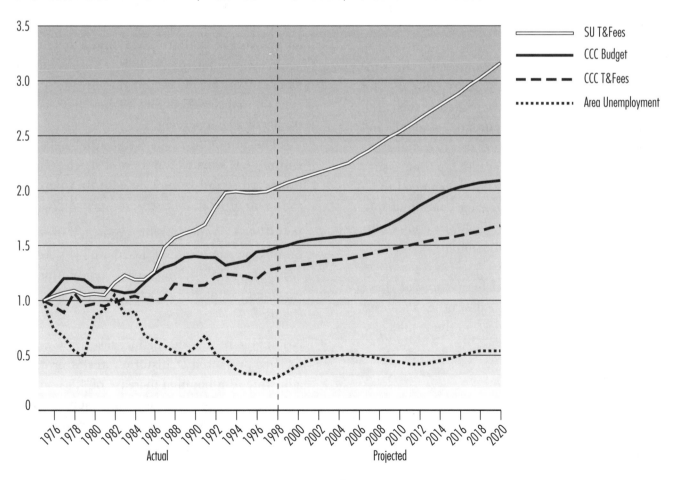

To illustrate this process, County CC in State A is again used as an example, and four relevant and possible scenarios are developed against a backdrop of basic, plausible assumptions:

- Scenario A: "status quo" or baseline, where historic trends external and internal to County CC continue.

- Scenario B: "industry relocation," where historic trends are disrupted by a major firm's departure from the city where County CC's main campus is located.

- Scenario C: "greater enrollment development," where County CC invests more resources in existing and new enrollment and marketing initiatives.

- Scenario D: "aggressive expansion" by County CC beyond its existing district service area.

To be most helpful to County CC, the ESP model is run separately for County CC's district and the outlying nondistrict areas. Research shows that the behavior of potential students and the demographics in each of the two areas are sufficiently different—as are the policy issues about each—that their consequences need to be separately analyzed before being combined into collegewide results. Many college situations warrant the use of segmented populations for the simulations.

A strength of the model is that any of these four scenarios may be modified or other scenarios posed in successive iterations, and the results easily reviewed.

Basic Assumptions

Underlying the work are certain basic assumptions about County CC and its service area:

- The general economic performance of County CC's service area—as reflected in revenue sources of the college's budget—is expected to be at about the same level over then next 18 years as it has been over the past 22 years. Increased productivity in area industries—from robotics and other technology—will maintain employment at historic levels (figure 8.1).

- Economic cycles are projected to be slightly longer, but less pronounced, in the future because of monetary and fiscal policies seeking stable and noninflationary growth. An economic downturn is projected in 1999 to 2005, an upswing in 2006 to 2012, and a downturn again beginning in 2013. Price inflation in County CC's area is projected to be 3 to 4 percent annually, only slightly higher than recent trends of 2 to 3 percent.

    The unemployment differential between County CC's district and nondistrict areas is projected to fall from 2 percent to 1 percent as the nondistrict area develops economically.

- Population growth will continue in the nondistrict outer area at about 1 percent annually, while the district population is expected to stabilize over the next two decades (figure 8.2).

- Nominal tuition and fee increases at County CC are projected at historic rates after price adjustment: a nominal increase of 4.5 percent —about $2 per credit unit each year— through 2005, and of 5 percent thereafter.

◆ After holding tuition and fees nearly constant since 1993, the nearby State University is expected to resume its earlier increases at a rate of about 1 percentage point per year greater than County CC's increases.

Forecasts, of course, rest not only on the effectiveness of the model but also on the eventual accuracy of the assumptions and projections. The assumptions used here appear reasonable and provide a useful backdrop for comparing the different consequences of the four scenarios.

Figure 8.2 Model Assumptions for County Community College Service Area Populations by County: Actual 1960–1995, Projected 1996–2020

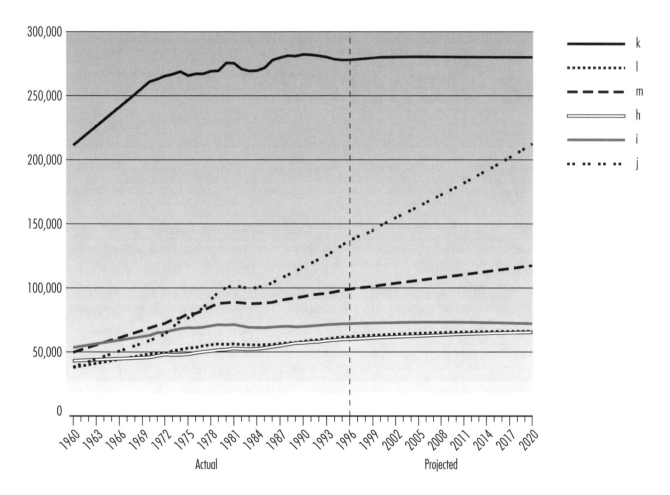

CHAPTER NINE

What Are Expected Enrollments under a Plausible Baseline Scenario?

The ESP model can be tested by constructing the "status quo" scenario, in which prior trends for key variables are extended into the future in ways that are plausible and, therefore, have some likelihood of actually taking place. Besides providing a test, this scenario can serve as a baseline against which the enrollment consequences of external "wild cards"—significant changes in college policy and practice (such as major increases in tuition and fees or delivery methods)—can be measured and compared.

This status quo scenario, A, results in rising County CC market penetration (E/P), with enrollment forecast to move gradually upward according to the assumed economic cycles. Thus, barring unexpected socioeconomic wild cards (like those in scenario B), County CC's market penetration and enrollment can be expected to increase even if the college makes few or no policy changes (figure 9.1). However, even over the next two decades, County CC's E/P only returns to its 1993 level, well below the consistently high years of 1977 to 1992, and possibly below goals

implied by the reasons that County CC's service to its community ought to increase (discussed in chapter 7).

Under scenario A, gains in market penetration by 2005 are greater in the outlying nondistrict areas (13 percent) than in County CC's district area (4 percent). If these trends were to continue, County CC's enrollment from the nondistrict areas would equal enrollment from the district areas by about 2030. This trend would be of little importance were it not that County CC is concerned about how to serve the outlying areas, and legislators in State A are concerned about access for such nondistrict territories.

As illustrated by County CC's case, despite a recent history of enrollment decline, probable future conditions in the college's service area should produce moderate enrollment increases even if the college makes no significant effort to improve its market penetration and restore enrollments. Consequently, college officials are interested in what would happen if they were to expand or to undertake a number of new initia-

Figure 9.1 County Community College Enrollment Results from Scenario A

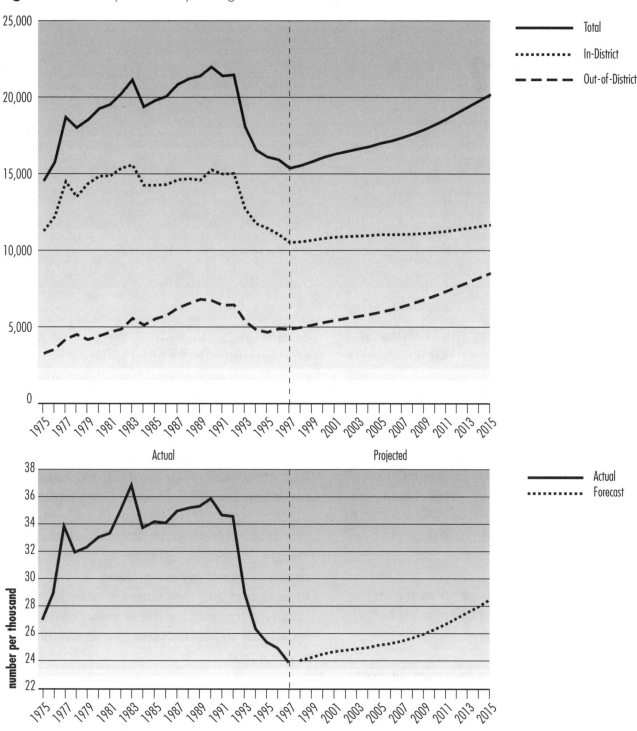

tives, or what would happen if the basic assumptions they have made do not hold. The ESP model is an ideal tool for examining such questions.

What If?

External future conditions in the baseline scenario described in chapter 9 may be changed within, for example, a likely or possible range, and the resulting enrollments forecast and analyzed. Manageable and unmanageable factors can be varied, in turn or simultaneously, in order to examine the consequences of different planning scenarios and to determine enrollment's sensitivity to possible policy changes. This chapter continues the illustrative story of County CC to examine three scenarios alternative to the baseline discussed in chapter 9.

Scenario B: What if a major firm leaves County CC's service area, disrupting the baseline trends in scenario A?

The arrival or departure of a major firm in a community college's service area, while outside the college's control, typically has a significant impact on enrollment.

The arrival of a new firm or the retooling of an existing firm can stimulate community college enrollment, particularly if the college has an arrangement with the firm (or the industry it's a part of) to train its labor force. In addition, the college gains tax base and typically experiences indirect budget improvements through increase in state-level aid.

A firm's departure also has an impact on college enrollment. Suppose that, for instance, a major local firm moves its production facilities out of the County CC service area in the years 2001 and 2002. This scenario, B, would substantially disrupt the local area economy, pushing unemployment up and population down in County CC's inner district area, and having a somewhat uncertain overall impact on the economy of the outer nondistrict areas. This scenario uses the following assumptions:

♦ The area's future population growth is similar to that in scenario A, except for a modest long-term decline in County CC's district area beginning in 2002.

◆ County CC's budget increases slowly between 2002 and 2006, as some of County's property tax base is lost and the regional economy adjusts, leaving County's revenue stream somewhat below that in scenario A.

◆ The area economic cycles described in scenario A are interrupted in 2001–02 as 14,000 inner-area workers are discharged. Another 10,000 regional workers are gradually discharged over the following five years because of indirect effects on suppliers and related industries.

◆ County CC and State University tuition and fees change at the same rates as in scenario A.

◆ Local inflation rates are unchanged from those in scenario A.

These assumed conditions in scenario B are quite different than those in scenario A (figure 10.1), but scenario B has a surprisingly modest overall effect on County CC's enrollment (figure 10.2). This is because the following effects cancel one another:

◆ Unemployment pushes County CC enrollment up as individuals seek job training.

◆ Budget reductions reduce County CC's ability to enroll more students.

◆ Population declines cause enrollment to decline in the long term.

> If the impact of unemployment on County CC's enrollment in this model is less than robust, as illustrated, this suggests that County CC needs to review its occupational offerings and delivery, and to assess the impact of other providers.

Figure 10.1 Model Assumptions for County Community College Budget, Area Population, and Unemployment, Scenarios A and B: 1998–2015

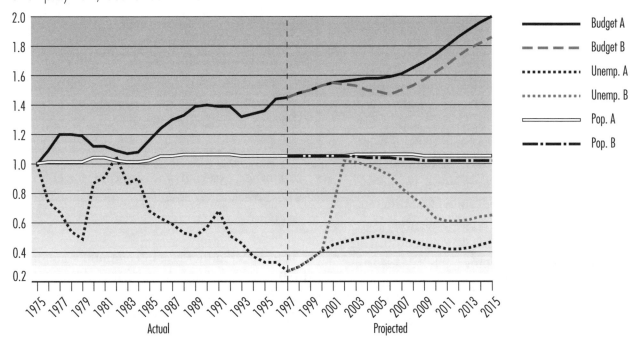

Thus, scenario B results in higher enrollment than scenario A in the short term—as the result of unemployment (though just 700 more at the 2002 peak), and in slightly lower enrollment than scenario A, beginning in 2007, as the result of budget and population decreases.

Scenario C: What if (where external conditions are like those in scenario A), County CC expands its enrollment development initiatives?

Scenario C returns to the external economic conditions assumed in scenario A—continuation of historic trends without any wild cards of the kind posed in scenario B—but adds expanded initiatives by County CC to increase its market penetration, particularly among residents who are

- enrolled, but not for any of County CC's published degrees or certificates

- immigrants

- welfare-to-work candidates

- recent high school graduates

- seeking higher or more technical skills

Under scenario C, County CC's existing initiatives to develop enrollments would be allocated additional resources. Efforts to partner with other educational providers and to expand the use of information technology (as in a "virtual college") would be accelerated. Counseling resources would be increased to provide "individual program packaging" for students seeking nondegree/non-certificate education; such packaging could use partners through outsourcing. These efforts would take place in the outlying nondistrict areas, as well as in the district areas near the main campus of County CC.

The following are assumed under scenario C:

- County CC budget changes are greater by five years of added investment for enrollment development, ranging from $0.6 million in 1999 to $4.0 million in 2003, for a total of $11 million added to the college's base funding.

> The source of funds for this budget increase is not clear. If funds were reallocated from other County CC functions, which might affect enrollments, the overall consequences would be uncertain.

- Development efforts cause budget elasticities of County CC enrollment (the response of potential students to program and service improvements) to triple for district residents and to double for nonresidents.

> Although assumptions about student response in the model appear reasonable, they must be considered as speculative, or perhaps as goals, because there is no empirical research available that identifies the enrollment impact of targeted marketing efforts in community colleges.

- All other external and internal variables in the forecasting model are unchanged from scenario A.

The expected increase in community and individual response that takes place under this scenario would add about 2,000 students each term to County CC's enrollment by 2005, and would

Figure 10.2 Model Results for County Community College Enrollments under Scenarios A and B: 1998–2015

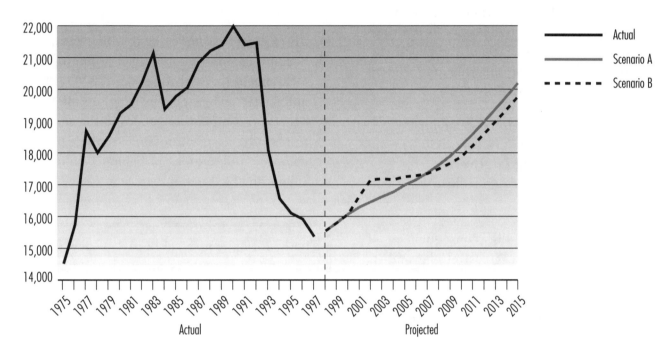

Figure 10.3 Model Results for County Community College Market Penetration under Scenarios A and C: 1998–2015

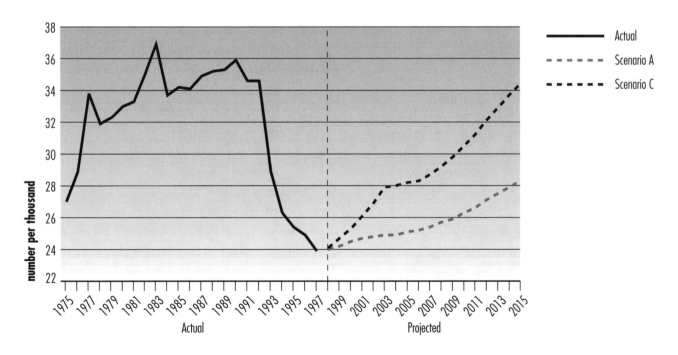

bring County CC's market penetration back to pre-1993 (reorganization) levels, but not until between 2010 and 2015, depending upon the development of the noncredit contract offerings (Figures 10.3 and 10.4). Half of the added students would be from the outlying nonresident areas of County CC's service area.

Scenario D: What if (where external conditions are like those in scenario A), County CC markets and delivers instruction to the outer region much more aggressively?

This scenario explores the consequences of County CC's expanding aggressively beyond its existing district borders into the adjacent outer areas that are not currently part of its legally defined district, or part of any other community college district in the state.

Scenario D assumes that

◆ Expansion of the County CC district takes place between 2000 and 2005 and annexes the territories of high school districts that are not now in County CC's district:

◇ all districts in counties k, l, and m (chapter 7)

◇ 7 of 17 districts in the outlying counties h, i, and j, where participation is highest. This includes 40 percent of the population in these three counties, nearly doubling County CC's district population base.

◆ Annexed populations

◇ are taxed for community college operations, enabling County CC to add $4 million per year to its budget for delivering instruction to residents of the outlying areas between 2000 and 2005

◇ have their student tuition and fees reduced to reflect their new district "resident" status

◆ Three centers (some or all of which eventually become campuses) are added at appropriate locations in the outlying areas in 2005, 2007, and 2010. (The specific locations of these centers is a topic that is beyond the scope of this study, as is discussion of the possible amounts and sources of capital funding for supporting facilities at the new sites.)

The historical empirical impact of new centers for County CC is minimal because of conflicting effects on the enrollment of nonresident students, most of whom (7 of 10) commute to the main campus, rather than attending at the centers. The potential impact of new centers or campuses can be estimated by looking at the effect of a center that opened in 1997 about 30 miles from the main campus. It added 1,000 enrollment (a change in E/P for nonresidents of +2.9/1000) during a period when nonresident enrollment declined by 10 percent. It seems reasonable to assume that new centers, properly located and sized, would have the same impact on market penetration, and we use this value in the forecast.

Under scenario D, County CC experiences significant increases in market penetration and enrollment once the annexations are underway. Enrollment of former nonresidents from the outlying areas grows rapidly and exceeds enrollment from the original resident district area by 2006 (figure 10.5).

Figure 10.4 Model Results for County Community College Enrollment under Scenarios A and C, by Residence: 1998–2015

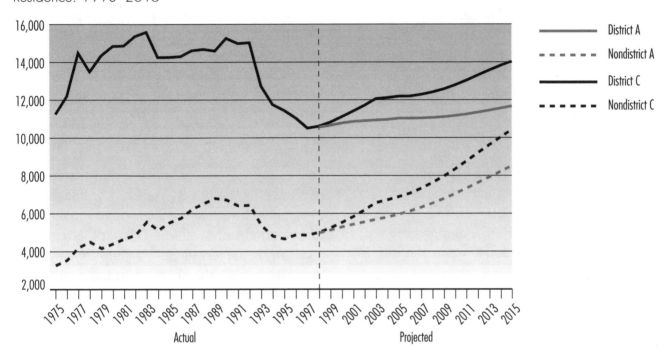

Figure 10.5 Model Results for County Community College Enrollment under Scenarios A and D, by Residence: 1998–2015

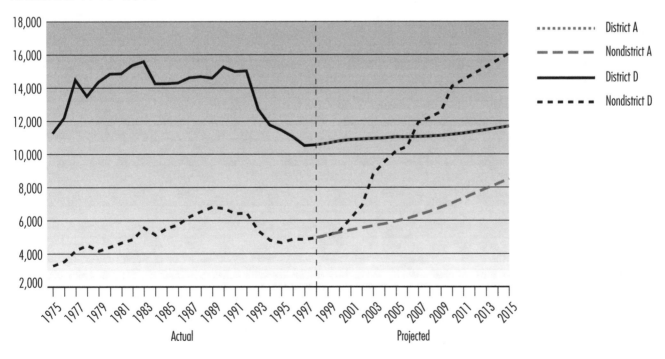

Nearly $20 million in operating funds for County CC are raised and go toward the cost of delivery in outlying areas. This investment lowers tuition and fees for about 40 percent of residents of the outlying areas, and the establishment of new County CC centers results in periodic jumps in County CC's penetration of these markets. Overall, scenario D brings County CC's market penetration back to pre-1993 levels by 2005.

How do forecasts from the different scenarios compare?

Enrollment forecasts from the four illustrated scenarios differ little until 2001, when the differences grow significantly:

Under the benchmark scenario A, where historic trends continue, County CC's market penetration and enrollment grow gradually. The eco-

nomic disruption caused by a major firm's departure from the metropolitan area (scenario B) exerts conflicting pressures on County CC's enrollments, increasing them in the short term and decreasing them over the long term. The net results from scenario B, on balance, differ little from those of scenario A in their magnitude, although an examination of student-body composition would most likely show some important differences.

Scenario C adds significant enrollment and improves market penetration, although the $11 million investment made is substantial and its source unclear. Scenario D conditions would result in the largest increase in enrollment, coming entirely from the nonresident outer region. It could only be accomplished by substantial reorganization efforts involving tax and annexation elections.

Figure 10.6 Model Results for County Community College Enrollment under Scenarios A, B, C, and D: 1998–2015

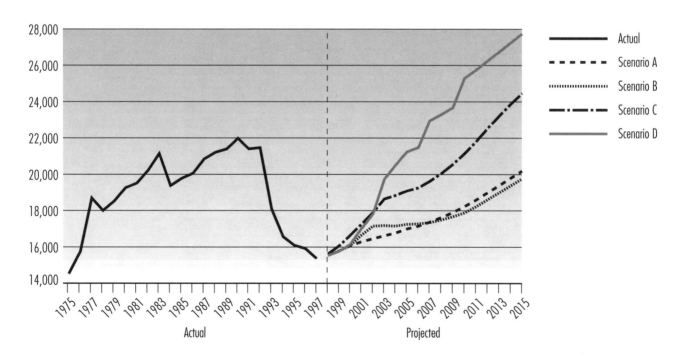

While there are an infinite number of other possible future scenarios that might effect County CC's planning, the above four represent those of most concern to the staff of County CC. In any case, the ESP model allows them to analyze most or all of the other possible options.

Table 10.1 County Community College Fall Enrollment of State A Residents

	Actual	Forecast		
	1997	2005	2010	2015
Scenario A	15,367	16,995	18,230	20,187
Scenario B	15,367	17,250	17,881	19,759
Scenario C	15,367	19,085	21,139	24,463
Scenario D	15,367	21,236	25,289	27,741

CHAPTER ELEVEN

What Are Some Important Trends and Wild Cards?

In order to build useful scenarios for the ESP model, college staff must make assumptions about future trends and events. The direction of service area demographics, economics, and prices are key to this work. This chapter discusses some of the current general trends; the importance of wild cards like wars, oil crises, strikes, earthquakes, and other hard-to-predict events; and community colleges' changing role.

Economic and Demographic Trends

It appears that the United States Federal Reserve Board plans to continue its policy goal of suppressing inflation, consistent with moderate growth (Greenspan 1998). Barring counterproductive fiscal policy, price inflation is not likely to increase much beyond recent trends, especially in the short term (the assumption in the illustrative scenario A).

Forecasts and related analyses note that the economic recovery that began in 1991 continues, but that it began to slow in 1998 because of Asian, Latin American, and Russian economic problems and a drawing down of U.S. inventories, and that it is slowing further in 1999. U.S. gross domestic product growth in 1999 is expected to be at least a full percentage point below the 1998 level. If so, this slowing of economic growth would be likely to increase the level of unemployment in most communities. In any case, it is doubtful that 1998's rate, close to 4 percent nationally, will go any lower, and it is likely to increase. As a result, demand for job training will continue to grow. Reports from the Information Technology Association (1997) show that 1 out of every 10 jobs in that industry go unfilled on a continuing basis. The search for foreign-trained labor to fill such gaps exceeds immigration limits each year. Greenspan's 1998 testimony notes that continuing U.S. economic growth could be limited by a lack of skills at all levels of the labor force.

Wild Cards

Unexpected events, referred to as wild cards in strategic planning, can be expected to occur. Extraordinary changes in economic conditions that alter demographic trends and community colleges' budgets and delivery capabilities can be modeled. For this purpose, alternative scenarios can be built to develop a probable range of enrollment forecasts, and to identify desired enrollment management strategies.

More difficult to analyze are events that may be one-time (war; rebuilding, retooling, or relocation of manufacturing plants); periodic (oil crises, strikes, earthquakes); or ongoing but subtle, at least at their onset (growth of proprietary higher education).

A wild card of major importance to County CC, embodied in scenario D, is a possible state-level policy to incorporate all of the state's territory into a community college district. A task force authorized by the state legislature was to report on how to do this. The extensive outlying areas surrounding County CC are a prominent part of this analysis because of their size and growing population.

Another one-time event is the upcoming turn of the century and the need to recode programs or change systems in order to keep calendar-related processes viable. While it is clear that the year 2000 (Y2K) problem must be corrected for many industries, neither the extent of the problem nor its possible impact on economic and social condi-

tions is clear; speculation on the possible impact ranges from nominal to catastrophic. The 1999 to 2001 conversion of European currencies to the Euro poses similarly uncertain, though indirect, consequences for community colleges.

An example of ongoing influences might be the increasing roles of proprietary postsecondary education and distributed electronic learning technologies.

Changing College Roles

Along with technological change and the changing roles of other providers, community colleges face uncertain changes to their missions and methods of operation brought about by the changing needs of society. The character of these changes is continuously debated. Some, like Daniel Moriarty (1996), argue that the changes will be evolutionary; others, like Richard Alfred and Patricia Carter (1996), argue that they should be revolutionary. Terry O'Banion (1997) makes the case for revolutionary change to a "learning college," where concepts of quality improvement and a focus on student customers involve learning that is collaborative, contextual, and flexible, and that embraces the useful aspects of information technology. As community colleges become involved in such changes, enrollment forecasting must be adjusted. The forecasting model recommended here, relying as heavily as it does on past relationships, can and should be modified accordingly.

In the example, County CC already uses technology (its "virtual college") and partnering (its trucking management program with the nearby State University), and is expanding its marketing among area high schools, among other new ways to provide for its student "customers." The extent of the effort that County CC made in these and other areas would significantly affect its future enrollments.

Also affecting community college enrollment forecasts are the unstructured markets described by Alfred and Carter (1997). The authors assert that community colleges must replace traditional market research and questions about courses and marketing with new practices and questions, such as, How fast, relevant and customized can instruction be? Efforts to provide more market-driven, customized, convenient, and technology-based instruction to new service areas—as in the case described for County CC—will cause community colleges' market view to change significantly.

CHAPTER TWELVE

Using Enrollment Simulation and Planning Modeling

A college must understand the simultaneous interaction of a complex set of variables on its enrollment; otherwise, changes initiated by the college may not have the expected results. For instance, large investments in marketing to increase enrollment may be thwarted if federal financial aid is decreasing and the college is raising tuition and fees at rates substantially greater than those of its competitors, or of prices generally.

This chapter suggests ways to prevent such unwanted outcomes and shows how the college staff can use enrollment simulation and planning modeling to achieve desired results and to plan strategically for an uncertain future.

ESP begins with focusing on a community college's student enrollment, including the causes for its fluctuation and possible future trends. But, as is shown in the chapter 11 illustration of County CC, this exercise causes staff to consider conditions that are external as well as internal to their college.

In the case of County CC, a major concern is the possible relocation of a major local industry. This concern is followed by interest in increasing marketing initiatives and in a possible reorganization of the college's service area. After the specification of some basic assumptions, the ESP model quickly simulates the enrollment consequences of these alternative scenarios and raises a number of additional questions about County CC's policies and practices. The model enables staff at County CC to simulate any number of other scenarios, reflecting different community conditions and different sets of proposed policies and practices. Figure 12.1 displays some of the kinds of useful observations and issues that can be derived from ESP. These statements and the forecasts illustrated in chapter 11 form a potent framework for effective strategic planning by County CC.

Slightly different concerns engage Metro CC. After four years of enrollment decline—the first such trend in its history—Metro outsourced a master plan study and began to consider a number of possible marketing efforts. The college is uncertain about what caused the recent enrollment downturn; is concerned about the specific character of marketing and curriculum change; and wonders how fast, and where, to establish two

Figure 12.1 Summary of Findings and Observations from ESP at County Community College

◆ Most of the past enrollment fluctuation at County Community College resulted from:

  ◇ the service area's economic cycles (unemployment)

  ◇ tuition and fee changes at County CC and nearby State University

  ◇ County CC's budget and curriculum changes

  ◇ area population trends

◆ An improved economy helped cause a recent enrollment decline at County CC. Some of the decline is the result of a curriculum reorganization; some may be the result of the college's "competitive edge."

◆ Findings from ESP are consistent with a County CC marketing study that shows that students consider County CC to be a "close and acceptable substitute" for the lower division at State University.

◆ Access is a major goal for County CC, and can be measured by market penetration (enrollment divided by population, or E/P). County CC's E/P has declined by one-third since 1990, but is still higher than the E/Ps of most other community colleges in its state and across the nation. The decline has been greatest among white students, so that the E/P for African American students (which is also down, but to a lesser extent) is now equal to that for white students.

◆ Market penetration at County CC appears to be holding up for younger, daytime, nonvocational, and out-of-district students but not holding up for older, evening, vocational, and in-district students.

◆ County CC's market penetration is likely to increase in the future because of increasing numbers of area high school graduates (to 2008) and an increasing unemployment rate in the area.

◆ Several factors argue for an increase in County CC's current market penetration:

  ◇ some restoration of access back to previously higher levels

  ◇ continual increases in technology and in the skills needed for jobs in the area

  ◇ changes to County CC's mission, possibly including a greater role in providing education for residents of the outlying areas, welfare-to-work program participants, and immigrants

or three new campuses. Metro CC is located in a community that continues to grow and the college wants to make its services available evenly across its entire service area.

Application of the ESP model and work with Metro's staff showed that several factors, including the neglect of evening occupational programming, had caused the enrollment decline. This supported the staff's interest in marketing and curriculum change. In addition, enrollment forecasts in Metro's prior master plan were based on the unrealistic assumption that the college's market penetration would be constant in the future. As figure 12.2 demonstrates, this condition had not occurred in Metro CC's nearly three decades of existence. Indeed, if Metro CC does little or nothing, its market penetration would likely increase because of external conditions. But initiatives already underway at Metro CC—marketing, curriculum revision, and a planned new cam-

pus center—will make the college's market penetration begin increasing from existing levels to prior levels.

Figure 12.2 displays two future scenarios for Metro CC. The first scenario (A) embodies plausible assumptions about the continuation of external conditions and projects plans for two new campus sites, opening in 2001 and 2010. The second scenario (B) embodies somewhat less favorable—for the college—trends in external conditions and the probable resulting delays in opening the new campuses. Both scenarios push market penetration above prior levels in the short term; scenario A, but not B, continues that level in the long term.

Thus, work with ESP provides Metro CC with valuable information for planning certain macro- and micro-policy changes that because of the college's circumstances, are different than the policy changes relevant to County CC.

Figure 12.2 Model Results for Metro Community College under Scenarios A and B, and Master Plan

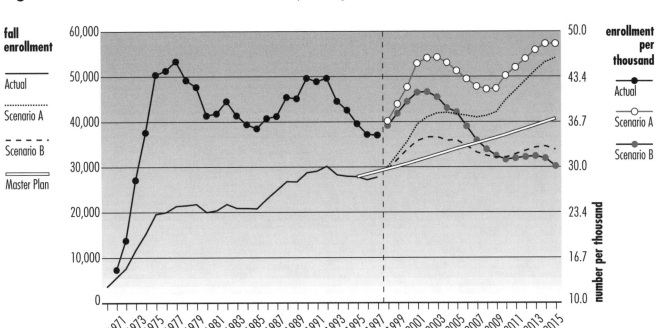

Data Requirements for Enrollment Simulation and Planning

These data are derived from multiple sources internal and external to the college, many of them found on the Internet.

The author recommends imputing data where they are missing or invalid if it would demonstrably improve the analysis.

Table 1. STUDENT DATA						
FTE by category	Credit, Headcount			Noncredit, Headcount	Gender	
	Total	Full-Time	Part-Time	Categories: Preparatory, Supplemental, Developmental, Tech/Prep, Apprentice, etc. (College-Defined)	Male	Female
1957* . . . 1980 . . . 1990 . . . 1998						

Table 2. STUDENT DATA								
Race and Ethnicity						Delivery		
African American	American Indian	Asian	Hispanic	White	Other	Off-Campus	Day	Evening
1957* . . . 1980 . . . 1990 . . . 1998								

Notes: *Or, whenever college started and/or data are available.

Headcount is unduplicated, generally for fall (though spring numbers would help). • FTE (full-time-equivalent) is usually annual, either credit- or contact hour-based (specify definition). • Noncredit categories as defined by colleges. • Day/evening distinction usually before/after 5 p.m.; also both if students attend both.

Table 3. STUDENT DATA								
Academic Goal				Load		Residence		
Transfer	Occup., Job Training	General Studies	Basic Skills	WSCH per FT	WSCH per PT	In Service Area	Other In-State	Non-resident
1957 . . . 1980 . . 1990 . . 1998								

Table 4. STUDENT DATA							
Status				Age	Education	Income	
New	Continuing	Returning	Transfer		Categories (College-Defined)	Self-Supporting	Dependent
1957 . . . 1980 . . 1990 . . 1998							

Notes: Elements and categories are defined by the colleges. Add any other student categories of importance to the colleges.

Table 5. PRICE OF COLLEGE							
Basic Tuition/Fees		Course, Other Fees		Student Financial Aid			Other Direct Costs
Posted	Revenues	Posted	Revenues	Federal	State	Local	Transportation, Books, Childcare, etc.
1957 · · · · 1980 · · · 1990 · · · 1998							

Note: Besides using "posted" rates, will try to derive actual rates from nominal revenues.

Table 6. INSTITUTIONAL POLICIES							
Curriculum		Support Services		College Budget $ Outlays			Other
Sections	Programs	Counseling	Marketing	Unrestricted E&G	Restricted E&G	Financial Aid, etc.	Factors Describing College
1957 · · · · 1980 · · · 1990 · · · 1998							

Note: Expenditures in nominal dollars.

Table 7. SERVICE AREA(S) DEMOGRAPHICS							
1957							
.							
.							
.		Here, we are looking for population characteristics that parallel those used for students:					
1980		gender					
.		race/ethnicity					
.		age					
.		income					
.		residence					
1990		etc., for the SAME college service area(s).					
.							
.							
1998							

Table 8. SERVICE AREA(S) ECONOMIC AND OTHER CONDITIONS						
Labor Market			Prices		Personal Income	Other, Non-Economic Conditions
Employed	Under-Employed	Not Employed	Local Consumer	College	Categories (College-Defined)	
1957						
.						
.			Here, we are looking for measures and conditions that affect the ability and interest of individuals to enroll; in some cases, it will be necessary to use proxies; in other cases, to impute missing data (if that improves the analysis).			
.						
1980						
.						
.						
.						
1990						
.						
1998						

Use of Linear Regression Model to Study Enrollment

Enrollment simulation and planning (ESP) uses a linear regression equation to analyze a community college's data and measure parameters that help explain and predict enrollment:

$$E = a + b_1F_X + b_2F_{SU} + b_3P + b_4UN + b_5B + b_6C + e$$

where E = student enrollment at Community College X

   F_X = College X's student tuition and fees

   F_{SU} = State University's student tuition and fees

   P = Population of College X's service area

   UN = Unemployment in College X's service area

   B = College X's operating budget

   C = College X's delivery

and

$a, b1, …, b6$ = regression parameters

   e = model estimate errors or "residuals"

The first step is to fit this model to historic data in order to estimate past enrollment patterns. Time series analyses like this typically have a high "fit" because most variables are increasing over time. Consequently, close attention is payed to the model's errors or residuals. For this, the *Durbin-Watson (DW) statistic* helps explain enrollment trends that result from factors not in the model by measuring the pattern of model errors or "residuals." The closer DW is to the value 2, the less likely it will be to have left out important factors.

Residuals may also be compared to actual enrollment to measure the relative *percent error* in the estimate for any given year or years.

Besides the model's overall fit, the relative impact on enrollment of the different factors or variables is assessed. In this case, two measures are especially useful:

♦ *Elasticity (e)* is the percent change in enrollment that results from a 1 percent change in an independent variable (such as fees or unemployment) when the impact on enrollment of other variables in the model is held constant

◆ *T-value (t)* indicates the significance or statistical "fit" of each variable—how well each is related—to enrollment. The t-value enables it to be said, for instance, at a standard 95 percent confidence level, that the probability (P) <0.01 means there is less than one chance in 100 that the results are due to purely random events.

Regression models may have certain inherent problems, or *model errors*. Independent variables may be highly interrelated, relationships may not be linear, important variables may be missing, or the direction of causation may not be clear. Valid study must identify and correct such problems as they occur.

Also contributing to potential errors are data problems or *measurement errors*. Some data may not measure what we think they do, may be measured incorrectly, or may be missing. There is no one simple rule to correct for such problems; they must be addressed as they are encountered.

The work described here can be performed in a modified spreadsheet created in Excel, Lotus, or other equivalent software program. Table B.1 shows one possible template for displaying results. A major advantage of using a spreadsheet, rather than a statistical utility like SAS or SPSS, is that once it has been modified to include the necessary statistics, the spreadsheet, provides easy access to powerful and attractive graphics for effective presentation to planners and policymakers.

Table B.1 Illustrative Display of Results from ESP Model

Durbin Watson Statistic = 1.991 | Significance = +no / − no

Regression:	t	P	Elasticity	Averages	
Enroll/Pop.				36.420	
Tuition & Fees	-5.426	0.000019	-0.69	$190.860	**Adj.R² = 0.906**
Unemploy.R.	5.140	0.000038	0.55	0.049	**F Ratio = 63.57**
Budget	6.071	0.000004	0.60	$45,816,056	
Sites	1.840	0.079246	0.17	4.330	

Correlations:	E/P	T&F	Unemploy.R.	Budget	Sites
Enroll/Pop.	1.000				
Tuition & Fees	0.014	1.000			
Unemploy.R	0.523	-0.472	1.000		
Budget	0.565	0.730	-0.267	1.000	
Sites	0.621	0.713	-0.008	0.871	1.000

Note: In the ESP software, the notations +yes or −yes indicate there is significant autocorrelation of forecast model errors in a positive or negative way. If there is no significant autocorrelation, the notations +no or −no are used.

Forecasting and Simulation Process

The author's work suggests a two-step, possibly three-step, forecasting process for ESP. First, a version of the econometric model in appendix B is used to forecast a college's future participation rate, $(E/P^\wedge)$. For Community College X, for instance:

$$E/P^\wedge = a + b_1 F_X + b_2 F_{SU} + b_3 B + b_4 C + b_5 D + b_6 U + u$$

where, F_X = College X's posted tuition and fees*

F_{SU} = Nearby State University tuition and fees*

B = X's general unrestricted operating budget*

C = delivery or policy variable(s) for College X if needed

D = College X's delivery (campus sites, etc.)

U = College X's service area Unemployment Rate

*Adjusted from nominal to real values by appropriate price indices.

Second, forecast fall credit enrollments $(E^\wedge)$ are derived by:

$$E^\wedge = (E/P^\wedge) * P^\wedge$$

where, $P^\wedge$ = forecasts of future service area population

And, in a possible *third* step of the recommended process, future full-time student equivalents $(FTE^\wedge)$ may be derived using the form:

$$FTE^\wedge = L^\wedge * E^\wedge$$

where, $L^\wedge$ = ratio of FTE/E, estimated and forecast either using the same independent variables used in step one; one of several curve-fitting techniques; or heuristic methods reflecting the expected consequence of programmatic, delivery, and enrollment changes on student academic loading.

This process, like the study of enrollment, can be conducted in a modified spreadsheet environment.

Bibliography

Alfred, Richard, and Patricia Carter. 1996. "Inside Track to the Future." *Community College Journal* (February/March).

———. 1997. "New Strategies for Organizational Development." *Community College Journal* (December/January).

American Association of Community Colleges. 1997. *AACC Annual 1997–98*. Washington, D.C.: Community College Press, American Association of Community Colleges.

Brinkman, Paul, Kurt Groninga, and Chuck McIntyre. 1994. *Computer-Aided Planning (CAP)*. Presentation at Annual Conference of Society for College and University Planning, San Francisco.

Brinkman, Paul, and Larry Leslie. 1987. "Student Price Response in Higher Education." *Journal of Higher Education* (March/April).

Brinkman, Paul, and Chuck McIntyre. 1997. "Methods and Techniques of Enrollment Forecasting." In *Forecasting and Managing Enrollment and Revenue: An Overview of Current Trends, Issues, and Methods*. Layzell, D., ed. *New Directions for Institutional Research* 93: 67-80. San Francisco: Jossey-Bass.

Brinkman, Paul, Chuck McIntyre, and Trische Robertson. 1995. *Computer-Aided Planning (CAP): Users Manual*. Sacramento, Calif.: Computer-Aided Planning.

California Community Colleges. 1993. *Study of Fee Impact: Phase 2, 1993*. ED 355 998. Sacramento, Calif.: Office of the Chancellor, Research and Analysis Unit.

———. 1996. *15-Year Enrollment and WSCH Forecast*. Sacramento, Calif.: Office of the Chancellor.

Dallas County Community College District. 1996. *Multi-Campus Community College System: Enrollment Penetration Study*. Dallas: Dallas County Community College District.

Dolence, Michael. 1993. *Strategic Enrollment Management: A Primer for Campus Administrators*. Washington, D.C.: American Association of Collegiate Registrars and Admissions Officers.

Drucker, Peter. 1967. *Managing for Results*. London: Pan Books.

Greenspan, Alan. 1998. *Quarterly Report to Congress on the Economy*. Washington, D.C.: U.S. Congress Joint Economic Committee.

Information Technology Association. 1997. *Help Wanted: The IT Workforce Gap at the Dawn of a New Century*. Washington, D.C.: AACC Commission Meetings.

Keller, George. 1983. *Academic Strategy: The Management Revolution in American Higher Education*. Baltimore: The Johns Hopkins University Press.

———. 1997. "Planning, Decisions, and Human Nature." *Planning for Higher Education* 26 (2): 18-24.

Kerr, Clark, et al. 1994. *Troubled Times for American Higher Education: The 1990s and Beyond*. SUNY Series: Frontiers in Education. Albany: State University of New York Press.

Lin, Y., and W. Vogt. 1996. "Occupational Outcomes for Students Earning Two-Year College Degrees: Income, Status, and Equity." *The Journal of Higher Education*, 67 (July/August), 446-460.

McIntyre, Chuck. 1982. "Price-Elasticity of Demand for Two-Year College Enrollment." Unpublished paper presented at the annual conference of the Western Economic Association, Los Angeles.

———. 1995. *Study of Tuition and Fees*. Study for Maricopa County Community College District. Sacramento, Calif.: Computer-Aided Planning.

———. 1997a. "Access to California Community Colleges." *A Technical Paper for the 2005 Task Force of the Chancellor's Consultation Council*. Sacramento, Calif.: Office of the Chancellor.

———. 1997b. "Trends Important to Community Colleges." *Core Issues in Community Colleges*. Washington, D.C.: American Association of Community Colleges and the Sloan Foundation.

———. 1998a. *Study of Enrollment*. Report prepared for Pima County Community College District. Sacramento, Calif.: Computer-Aided Planning.

———. 1998b. *LCC Enrollment Simulation and Planning*. Study for Lansing Community College. Sacramento, Calif.: Computer-Aided Planning.

———. 1998c. *Enrollment Simulation and Planning at Lane Community College: Preliminary Report*. Study for Lane Community College. Sacramento, Calif.: Computer-Aided Planning.

———. 1998d. *PCC Enrollment Simulation and Planning: Preliminary Report*. Study for Portland Community College. Sacramento, Calif.: Computer-Aided Planning.

Moriarty, Daniel. 1996. "In Rough Seas, Stay the Course." *Community College Journal* (February/March).

Nedwek, Brian. 1998. "Organizational Transformation Begins with You." *Planning for Higher Education* 26 (4): 31-36.

O'Banion, Terry. 1997. *A Learning College for the 21st Century*. Phoenix: Oryx Press.

Schmidtlein, George. 1990. "Why Linking Budgets to Plans Has Proven Difficult in Higher Education." *Planning for Higher Education* 18 (2): 9-23.

Index

About the Author

Chuck McIntyre is the director of research and analysis at the State Chancellor's Office of the California Community Colleges. He has more than 31 years of experience in higher education planning, research, evaluation, finance, and management. He has helped develop several long-range plans for the California Board of Governors, and he has worked on enrollment forecasting, simulation, and management projects for a number of colleges in California and other states. McIntyre has written several books and articles on college planning, and he directs workshops and symposia and speaks about planning at national conferences. He holds a Ph.D. and an M.A. in economics and a B.A. in anthropology. He has taught undergraduate microeconomics and graduate higher education finance at California State University.